Fifth International Workshop on Natural Language Processing for Social Media (SocialNLP 2017)

AA001540

Valencia, Spain
3 April 2017

ISBN: 978-1-5108-3871-0

Printed from e-media with permission by:

Curran Associates, Inc.
57 Morehouse Lane
Red Hook, NY 12571

Some format issues inherent in the e-media version may also appear in this print version.

Copyright© (2017) by the Association for Computational Linguistics
All rights reserved.

Printed by Curran Associates, Inc. (2017)

For permission requests, please contact the Association for Computational Linguistics
at the address below.

Association for Computational Linguistics
209 N. Eighth Street
Stroudsburg, Pennsylvania 18360

Phone: 1-570-476-8006
Fax: 1-570-476-0860

acl@aclweb.org

Additional copies of this publication are available from:

Curran Associates, Inc.
57 Morehouse Lane
Red Hook, NY 12571 USA
Phone: 845-758-0400
Fax: 845-758-2633
Email: curran@proceedings.com
Web: www.proceedings.com

SocialNLP@EACL2017 Chairs' Welcome

It is our great pleasure to welcome you to the Fifth International Workshop on Natural Language Processing for SocialMedia-SocialNLP 2017, associated with EACL 2017. SocialNLP is an inter-disciplinary area of natural language processing (NLP) and social computing. We hold SocialNLP twice a year: one in the NLP venue, the other in the associated venue such as those for web technology or artificial intelligence. There are three plausible directions of SocialNLP: (1) addressing issues in social computing using NLP techniques; (2) solving NLP problems using information from social media; and (3) handling new problems related to both social computing and natural language processing. Through this workshop, we anticipate to provide a platform for research outcome presentation and head-to-head discussion in the area of SocialNLP, with the hope to combine the insight and experience of prominent researchers from both NLP and social computing domains to contribute to the area of SocialNLP jointly. The submissions to this year's workshop were again of high quality and we had a competitive selection process. We received 13 submissions from Asia, Europe, and the United States, and due to a rigorous review process, we only accepted 6 long oral papers. Thus the acceptance rate was 46 percent. Compared to the recent workshops in United States, the submission number is a bit small. This also encourages us to have more related activities in Europe to expand our community here.

This year, we are delighted to have Prof. Dirk Hovy, from the University of Copenhagen, as our keynote speaker. We also encourage attendees to attend the keynote and invited talk presentation to have more discussions with outstanding researchers. Their valuable and insightful talk can and will guide us to a better understanding of the future. Putting together SocialNLP 2017 was a team effort. We first thank the authors for providing the quality content of the program. We are grateful to the program committee members, who worked very hard in reviewing papers and providing feedback for authors. Finally, we especially thank the Workshop Committee Chairs Prof. Laura Rimell and Prof. Richard Johansson.

We hope you join our community and enjoy the workshop!

Organizers

Lun-Wei Ku, Academia Sincia, Taiwan
Cheng-Te Li, National Cheng Kung University, Taiwan

Organizers

Lun-Wei Ku, Academia Sincia, Taiwan
Cheng-Te Li, National Cheng Kung University, Taiwan

Program Committee:

Tim Althoff, Stanford University
Sabine Bergler, Concordia University
Berlin Chen, National Taiwan Normal University
Hsin-Hsi Chen, National Taiwan University
Hai Leong Chieu, DSO National Laboratories
Monojit Choudhury, Microsoft Research
Freddy Chua, Singapore Management University
Nigel Collier, University of Cambridge
Danilo Croce, University of Roma, Tor Vergata
Lei Cui, Microsoft Research
Ronan Cummins, University of Cambridge
Pradipto Das, Rakuten USA
Min-Yuh Day, Tamkang University, Taiwan
Ann Devitt, Trinity College Dublin
Eduard Dragut, Temple University
Koji Eguchi, Kobe University
Michael Elhadad, Ben-Gurion University
Wei Gao, Qatar Computing Research Institute
Spandana Gella, University of Edinburgh
Marco Guerini, Fondazione Bruno Kessler
Weiwei Guo, LinkedIn
William Hamilton, Stanford University
Graeme Hirst, University of Toronto
Wen-Lian Hsu, Academia Sinica
Diana Inkpen, University of Ottawa
David Jurgens, Stanford University
Pallika Kanani, Oracle Labs
Soo-Min Kim, Amazon
Roman Klinger, University of Stuttgart
June-Jei Kuo, National Chung Hsing University
Tsung-Ting Kuo, University of California, San Diego
Cheng-Te Li, National Cheng Kung University
Chuan-Jie Lin, National Taiwan Ocean University
Shou-De Lin, National Taiwan University
Yiqun Liu, Tsinghua University
Zhiyuan Liu, Tsinghua University
Bin Lu, Google Inc.
Zhunchen Luo, China Defense Science and Technology Information Center
Bruno Martins, University of Lisbon
Yelena Mejova, Qatar Computing Research Institute
Rada Mihalcea, University of Michigan
Manuel Montes-y-Gómez, INAOE, Mexico

Dong Nguyen, University of Twente
Haris Papageorgiou, ATHENA Research and Innovation Center
Souneil Park, Telefonica Research
Michael Paul, University of Colorado Boulder
Georgios Petasis, NCSR "Demokritos"
Stephen Pulman, Oxford University
Sravana Reddy, Wellesley College
Paolo Rosso, Universitat Politècnica de València
Derek Ruths, McGill University
Saurav Sahay, Intel Labs
Hassan Saif, The Open University
Yohei Seki, University of Tsukuba
Mário J. Silva, Universidade de Lisboa
Yanchuan Sim, Institute for Infocomm Research
Jan Snajder, University of Zagreb
Jannik Strötgen, Max Planck Institute for Informatics
Xavier Tannier, Université Paris-Sud, LIMSI, CNRS
Mike Thelwall, University of Wolverhampton
Ming-Feng Tsai, National Chengchi University
Paola Velardi, Università di Roma
Marc Verhagen, Brandeis University
Svitlana Volkova, PNNL
Xiaojun Wan, Peking University
Hsin-Min Wang, Academia Sinica
Jenq-Haur Wang, National Taipei University of Technology
William Yang Wang, UC Santa Barbara
Ingmar Weber, Qatar Computing Research Institute, HBKU
Robert West, École Polytechnique Fédérale de Lausanne
Kam-Fai Wong, The Chinese University of Hong Kong
Shih-Hung Wu, Chaoyang University of Technology
Ruifeng Xu, Harbin Institute of Technology
Yi Yang, Georgia Tech
Liang-Chih Yu, Yuan Ze University
Zhe Zhang, IBM Watson
Hua-Ping Zhang, Beijing Institute of Technology
Ming Zhou, Microsoft Research Asia
Deyu Zhou, Southeast University

Table of Contents

Conference Program

09:30–09:40 Opening

09:40–10:50 *Keynote Speech 1: NLP, the perfect social (media) science?*
Prof. Dirk Hovy, the University of Copenhagen

10:50–11:20 Coffee Break

11:20–12:10 *A Survey on Hate Speech Detection using Natural Language Processing*
Anna Schmidt and Michael Wiegand

12:10–12:40 *Facebook sentiment: Reactions and Emojis*
Ye Tian, Thiago Galery, Giulio Dulcinati, Emilia Molimpakis and Chao Sun

12:40–13:10 *Potential and Limitations of Cross-Domain Sentiment Classification*
Jan Milan Deriu, Martin Weilenmann, Dirk Von Gruenigen and Mark Cieliebak

14:20–15:30 *Keynote Speech 2*

15:30–16:20 Coffee Break/Poster Session

16:20–16:50 *Aligning Entity Names with Online Aliases on Twitter*
Kevin McKelvey, Peter Goutzounis, Stephen da Cruz and Nathanael Chambers

16:50–17:20 *Character-based Neural Embeddings for Tweet Clustering*
Svitlana Vakulenko, Lyndon Nixon and Mihai Lupu

17:20–17:50 *A Twitter Corpus and Benchmark Resources for German Sentiment Analysis*
Mark Cieliebak, Jan Milan Deriu, Dominic Egger and Fatih Uzdilli

A Survey on Hate Speech Detection using Natural Language Processing

Anna Schmidt
Spoken Language Systems
Saarland University
D-66123 Saarbrücken, Germany
anna.schmidt@lsv.uni-saarland.de

Michael Wiegand
Spoken Language Systems
Saarland University
D-66123 Saarbrücken, Germany
michael.wiegand@lsv.uni-saarland.de

Abstract

This paper presents a survey on hate speech detection. Given the steadily growing body of social media content, the amount of online hate speech is also increasing. Due to the massive scale of the web, methods that automatically detect hate speech are required. Our survey describes key areas that have been explored to automatically recognize these types of utterances using natural language processing. We also discuss limits of those approaches.

1 Introduction

Hate speech is commonly defined as any communication that disparages a person or a group on the basis of some characteristic such as race, color, ethnicity, gender, sexual orientation, nationality, religion, or other characteristic (Nockleby, 2000). Examples are (1)-(3).[1]

(1) Go fucking kill yourself and die already useless ugly pile of shit scumbag.
(2) The Jew Faggot Behind The Financial Collapse
(3) Hope one of those bitches falls over and breaks her leg

Due to the massive rise of user-generated web content, in particular on social media networks, the amount of hate speech is also steadily increasing. Over the past years, interest in online hate speech detection and particularly the automatization of this task has continuously grown, along with the societal impact of the phenomenon. Natural language processing focusing specifically on this phenomenon is required since basic word filters do not provide a sufficient remedy: What is considered a hate speech message might be influenced by aspects such as the domain of an utterance, its discourse context, as well as context consisting of co-occurring media objects (e.g. images, videos, audio), the exact time of posting and world events at this moment, identity of author and targeted recipient.

This paper provides a short, comprehensive and structured overview of automatic hate speech detection, and outlines the existing approaches in a systematic manner, focusing on feature extraction in particular. It is mainly aimed at NLP researchers who are new to the field of hate speech detection and want to inform themselves about the state of the art.

2 Terminology

In this paper we use the term ***hate speech***. We decided in favour of using this term since it can be considered a broad umbrella term for numerous kinds of insulting user-created content addressed in the individual works we summarize in this paper. *Hate speech* is also the most frequently used expression for this phenomenon, and is even a legal term in several countries. Below we list other terms that are used in the NLP community. This should also help readers with finding further literature on that task.

In the earliest work on hate speech, Spertus (1997) refers to *abusive* messages, *hostile* messages or *flames*. More recently, many authors have shifted to employing the term *cyberbullying* (Xu et al., 2012; Hosseinmardi et al., 2015; Zhong et al., 2016; Van Hee et al., 2015; Dadvar et al., 2013; Dinakar et al., 2012). The actual term *hate speech* is used by Warner and Hirschberg (2012), Burnap and Williams (2015), Silva et al. (2016), Djuric et al. (2015), Gitari et al. (2015), Williams and Burnap (2015) and Kwok and Wang (2013). Further,

[1]The examples in this work are included to illustrate the severity of the hate speech problem. They are taken from actual web data and in no way reflect the opinion of the authors.

Proceedings of the Fifth International Workshop on Natural Language Processing for Social Media, pages 1–10, Valencia, Spain, April 3-7, 2017. ©2017 Association for Computational Linguistics

Sood et al. (2012a) work on detecting (personal) *insults*, *profanity* and user posts that are characterized by *malicious intent*, while Razavi et al. (2010) refer to *offensive language*. Xiang et al. (2012) focus on *vulgar* language and *profanity-related offensive content*. Xu et al. (2012)[2] further look into jokingly formulated *teasing* in messages that represent (possibly less severe) bullying episodes. Finally, Burnap and Williams (2014) specifically look into *othering language*, characterized by an us-them dichotomy in racist communication.

3 Features for Hate Speech Detection

As is often the case with classification-related tasks, one of the most interesting aspects distinguishing different approaches is which features are used. Hate speech detection is certainly no exception since what differentiates a hateful speech utterance from a harmless one is probably not attributable to a single class of influencing aspects. While the set of features examined in the different works greatly varies, the classification methods mainly focus on supervised learning (§6).

3.1 Simple Surface Features

For any text classification task, the most obvious information to utilize are surface-level features, such as bag of words. Indeed, unigrams and larger n-grams are included in the feature sets by a majority of authors (Chen et al., 2012; Xu et al., 2012; Warner and Hirschberg, 2012; Sood et al., 2012b; Burnap and Williams, 2015; Van Hee et al., 2015; Waseem and Hovy, 2016; Burnap and Williams, 2016; Hosseinmardi et al., 2015; Nobata et al., 2016). These features are often reported to be highly predictive. Still, in many works n-gram features are combined with a large selection of other features. For example, in their recent work, Nobata et al. (2016) report that while token and character n-gram features are the most predictive single features in their experiments, combining them with all additional features further improves performance.

Character-level n-gram features might provide a way to attenuate the spelling variation problem often faced when working with user generated comment text. For instance, the phrase *kill yrslef a$$hole*, which is regarded as an example of hate speech, will most likely pose problems to token-based approaches since the unusual spelling variations will result in very rare or even unknown tokens in the training data. Character-level approaches, on the other hand, are more likely to capture the similarity to the canonical spelling of these tokens. Mehdad and Tetreault (2016) systematically compare character n-gram features with token n-grams for hate speech detection, and find that character n-grams prove to be more predictive than token n-grams.

Apart from word- and character-based features, hate speech detection can also benefit from other surface features (Chen et al., 2012; Nobata et al., 2016), such as information on the frequency of URL mentions and punctuation, comment and token lengths, capitalization, words that cannot be found in English dictionaries, and the number of non-alpha numeric characters present in tokens.

3.2 Word Generalization

While bag-of-words features usually yield a good classification performance in hate speech detection, in order to work effectively these features require predictive words to appear in both training and test data. However, since hate speech detection is usually applied on small pieces of text (e.g. passages or even individual sentences), one may face a data sparsity problem. This is why several works address this issue by applying some form of *word generalization*. This can be achieved by carrying out word clustering and then using induced cluster IDs representing sets of words as additional (generalized) features. A standard algorithm for this is *Brown clustering* (Brown et al., 1992) which has been used as a feature in Warner and Hirschberg (2012). While Brown clustering produces hard clusters – that is, it assigns each individual word to one particular cluster – *Latent Dirichlet Allocation (LDA)* (Blei et al., 2003) produces for each word a topic distribution indicating to which degree a word belongs to each topic. Such information has similarly been used for hate speech detection (Xiang et al., 2012; Zhong et al., 2016).

More recently, distributed word representations (based on neural networks), also referred to as *word embeddings*, have been proposed for a similar purposes. For each word a vector representation is induced (Mikolov et al., 2013) from a large (unlabelled) text corpus. Such vector representations have the advantage that different, semanti-

[2]The data from this work are available under `http://research.cs.wisc.edu/bullying`

cally similar words may also end up having similar vectors. Such vectors may eventually be used as classification features, replacing binary features indicating the presence or frequency of particular words. Since in hate speech detection sentences or passages are classified rather than individual words, a vector representation of the *set* of word vectors representing the words of the text to be classified is sought. A simple way to accomplish this is by averaging the vectors of all words occurring in one passage or sentence. For detecting hate speech, this method is only reported to have limited effectiveness (Nobata et al., 2016), no matter whether general pretrained embeddings are used or the embeddings are induced from a domain-specific corpus. Alternatively, Djuric et al. (2015) propose to use embeddings that directly represent the text passages to be classified. These *paragraph embeddings* (Le and Mikolov, 2014), which are internally based on word embeddings, have been shown to be much more effective than the averaging of word embeddings (Nobata et al., 2016).

3.3 Sentiment Analysis

Hate speech and sentiment analysis are closely related, and it is safe to assume that usually negative sentiment pertains to a hate speech message. Because of this, several approaches acknowledge the relatedness of hate speech and sentiment analysis by incorporating the latter as an auxiliary classification. Dinakar et al. (2012), Sood et al. (2012b) and Gitari et al. (2015) follow a multi-step approach, in which a classifier dedicated to detect negative polarity is applied prior to the classifier specifically checking for evidence of hate speech. Further, Gitari et al. (2015) run an additional classifier that weeds out non-subjective sentences prior to the aforementioned polarity classification.

Apart from multi-step approaches, there are also single-step approaches that include some form of sentiment information as a feature. For example, in their supervised classifier, Van Hee et al. (2015) use as features the number of positive, negative, and neutral words (according to a sentiment lexicon) occurring in a given comment text.

Further attempts to isolate the subset of hate speech from the set of negative polar utterances rest on the observation that hate speech also displays a *high degree* of negative polarity (Sood et al., 2012b; Burnap et al., 2013). To that end, polarity classifiers are employed which in addition to specifying the type of polarity (i.e. *positive* and *negative*) also predict the polar intensity of an utterance. A publicly available polarity classifier which produces such an output is *SentiStrength* (Thelwall et al., 2010). It is used for hate speech detection by Burnap et al. (2013).

3.4 Lexical Resources

Trying to make use of the general assumption that hateful messages contain specific negative words (such as slurs, insults, etc.), many authors utilize the presence of such words as a feature. To obtain this type of information lexical resources are required that contain such predictive expressions.

A popular source for such word lists is the web. There are several publicly available lists that consist of *general* hate-related terms.[3] Apart from works that employ such lists (Xiang et al., 2012; Burnap and Williams, 2015; Nobata et al., 2016), there are also approaches, such as Burnap and Williams (2016) which focus on lists that are *specialized* towards a particular subtype of hate speech, such as ethnic slurs[4], LGBT slang terms[5], or words with a negative connotation towards handicapped people.[6]

Apart from publicly-available word lists from the web other approaches incorporate lexicons that have been specially compiled for the task at hand. Spertus (1997) employs a lexicon comprising so-called *good verbs* and *good adjectives.* Razavi et al. (2010) manually compiled an *Insulting and Abusing Language Dictionary* containing both words and phrases with different degrees of manifestation of flame varieties. This dictionary also assigns weights to each lexical entry which represents the degree of the potential impact level for hate speech detection. The weights are obtained by *adaptive learning* using the training partition of the data set used in that work. Gitari et al. (2015) build a resource comprising *hate verbs* which are verbs that condone or encourage acts of violence. Despite their general effectiveness, rel-

[3] www.noswearing.com/dictionary, www.rsdb.org, www.hatebase.org

[4] https://en.wikipedia.org/wiki/List_of_ethnic_slurs

[5] https://en.wikipedia.org/wiki/List_of_LGBT_slang_terms

[6] https://en.wikipedia.org/wiki/List_of_disability-related_terms_with_negative_connotations

atively little is known about the creation process and the theoretical concepts that underlie the lexical resources that have been specially compiled for hate speech detection.

Most approaches employ lexical features either as some baseline or in addition to other features. In contrast to other features, particularly bag of words (§3.1) or embeddings (§3.2), they are usually insufficient as a stand-alone feature (Nobata et al., 2016). Contextual factors play an important role. For example, Hosseinmardi et al. (2015) find that 48% of media sessions in their data collection were not deemed hate speech by a majority of annotators, even though they reportedly contained a high percentage of profanity words.

3.5 Linguistic Features

Linguistic aspects also play an important role for hate speech detection. Linguistic features are either employed in a more generic fashion or are specifically tailored to the task.

Xu et al. (2012) explore the combination of ngram features with POS-information-enriched tokens. However, adding POS information does not significantly improve classifier performance.

Taking into account deeper syntactic information as a feature, Chen et al. (2012) employ typed dependency relationships. Such relationships have the potential benefit that non-consecutive words bearing a (potentially long-distance) relationship can be captured in one feature. For instance, in (4) a dependency tuple `nsubj(pigs, Jews)` will denote the relation between the offensive term *pigs* and the hate-target *Jews*.

(4) Jews are lower class pigs.

Obviously, knowing that those two words are syntactically related makes the underlying statement more likely to convey hate speech than those keywords occurring in a sentence without any syntactic relation. Dependency relationships are also employed in the feature set from Gitari et al. (2015), Burnap and Williams (2015), Burnap and Williams (2016) and Nobata et al. (2016). Burnap and Williams (2015) and Burnap and Williams (2016) report significant performance improvements based on this feature; the other papers do not conduct ablation studies from which one could conclude the effectiveness of this particular feature. There is also a difference in the sets of dependency relationships representing a sentence which are used. Burnap and Williams (2015) apply some statistical feature selection (*Bayesian Logistic Regression*), Chen et al. (2012) and Gitari et al. (2015) manually select the relations (e.g. by enforcing that one argument of the relation is an offensive term) while Nobata et al. (2016) do not carry out any further selection. Unfortunately, there does not exist any evaluation comparing these feature variations. Zhong et al. (2016) do not use the presence of explicit dependency relations occurring in a sentence as a feature but employ an *offensiveness level score*. This score is based on the frequency of co-occurrences of offensive terms and user identifiers in the same dependency relation.

In her work on the *Smokey* system, Spertus (1997) devises a set of linguistic features tailored to the task of hate speech detection. The syntactic features include the detection of *imperative* statements (e.g. *Get lost!*, *Get a life!*) and the co-occurrence of the pronoun *you* modified by noun phrases (as in *you bozos*). The *Smokey* system also incorporates some semantic features to prevent false positives. On the one hand, so-called *praise rules* are employed, which use regular expressions involving pre-defined *good words*. Since that work categorizes webpages, the praise rules try to detect co-occurrences of good words and expressions referring to the website to be classified. On the other hand, Spertus (1997) also employs *politeness rules* represented by certain polite words or phrases (e.g. *no thanks*, *would you* or *please*). Nobata et al. (2016) use a similar feature.

3.6 Knowledge-Based Features

Hate speech detection is a task that cannot be solved by simply looking at keywords. Even if one tries to model larger textual units, as researchers attempt to do by means of linguistic features (§3.5), it remains difficult to decide whether some utterance represents hate speech or not. For instance, (5) may not be regarded as some form of hate speech when only read in isolation.

(5) Put on a wig and lipstick and be who you really are.

However, when the context information is given that this utterance has been directed towards a boy on a social media site for adolescents[7], one could infer that this is a remark to malign the sexuality or gender identity of the boy being addressed (Dinakar et al., 2012). (5) displays stereotypes most

[7]The example utterance from above is from Formspring.

commonly attributed to females (i.e. *putting on a wig and lipstick*). If these characteristics are attributed to a male in a heteronormative context, the intention may have been to insult the addressee.

The above example shows that whether a message is hateful or benign can be highly dependent on world knowledge, and it is therefore intuitive that the detection of a phenomenon as complex as hate speech might benefit from including information on aspects not directly related to language. Dinakar et al. (2012) present an approach employing automatic reasoning over world knowledge focusing on anti-LGBT hate speech. The basis of their model is the general-purpose ontology *ConceptNet* (Liu and Singh, 2004), which encodes concepts that are connected by relations to form assertions, such as *"a skirt is a form of female attire"*. *ConceptNet* is augmented by a set of stereotypes (manually) extracted from the social media network *Formspring*.[8] An example for such a stereotype assertion is *"lipstick is used by girls"*. The augmented knowledge base is referred to as *BullySpace*.[9] This knowledge base allows computing the similarity of concepts of common knowledge with concepts expressed in user comments.[10] After extracting concepts present in a given user comment, the similarity between the extracted concepts and a set of four *canonical concepts* is computed. Canonical concepts are the four reference concepts *positive* and *negative valence* and the two genders, *male* and *female*. The resulting similarity scores between extracted and canonical concepts indicate whether a message might constitute a hate speech instance. A hate speech instance has a high similarity to the canonical concept *negative valence* and the canonical concept representing the gender opposed to the actual gender of the user being addressed in the message post. For example, for the sentence given above, a high similarity to *negative valence* and *female* would correctly indicate that the utterance is meant as hate speech.

Obviously, the approach proposed by Dinakar et al. (2012) only works for a very confined subtype of hate speech (i.e. anti-LGBT bullying). Even though the framework would also allow for other types of hate speech, it would require domain-specific assertions to be included first. This would require a lot of manual coding. It is presumably this shortcoming that explains why, to our knowledge, this is the only work that tries to detect hate speech with the help of a knowledge base.

3.7 Meta-Information

World knowledge gained from knowledge bases is not the only information available to refine inconclusive classification. Meta-information (i.e. information *about* an utterance) is also a valuable source to hate speech detection. Since the text commonly used as data for this task almost exclusively comes from social media platforms, a variety of such meta-information is usually offered and can be easily accessed via the APIs those platforms provide.

Having some background information about the user of a post may be very predictive. A user who is known to write hate speech messages may do so again. A user who is not known to write such messages is unlikely to do so in future. Xiang et al. (2012) effectively employ this heuristic in inferring further hate speech messages. Dadvar et al. (2013) use as a feature the number of profane words in the message history of a user. Knowing the gender of the user may also help (Dadvar et al., 2012; Waseem and Hovy, 2016). Men are much more likely to post hate speech messages than women.

Beyond these, several other kinds of meta-information are common, such as the number of posts by a user, the number of replies to a post, the average of the total number of replies per follower or the geographical origin, but most of these have not been found effective for classification (Zhong et al., 2016; Waseem and Hovy, 2016). Moreover, there are certain kinds of meta-information for which conflicting results have been reported. For instance, Hosseinmardi et al. (2015) report a correlation between the number of associated comments to a post and hate speech while Zhong et al. (2016) report the opposite. (Both papers use Instagram as a source.) Many reasons may be responsible for that. Zhong et al. (2016) speculate that the general lack in effectiveness of the meta-information they examined may be due to the fact they consider celebrity accounts. Accounts from regular users, on the other hand, may display quite a different behaviour. From that we conclude that

[8]The augmentation is achieved by applying the joint inference technique *blending* after both *ConceptNet* and the assertions have been transformed into a so-called *AnalogySpace*.

[9]*BullySpace* contains 200 LGBT-specific assertions.

[10]Concepts are represented as vectors, so the similarity can be easily computed by measures such as cosine-similarity.

meta-information may be helpful but it depends on the exact type of information one employs and also the source from which the data originate.

3.8 Multimodal Information

Modern social media do not only consist of text but also include images, video and audio content. Such non-textual content is also regularly commented on, and therefore becomes part of the discourse of a hate speech utterance. This context outside a written user comment can be used as a predictive feature.

As for knowledge-based features, not too many contributions exist that exploit this type of information. This is slightly surprising, since among hateful user posts illustrated by websites documenting representative cases of severe cyber hate[11], visual context plays a major role.

Hosseinmardi et al. (2015) employ features based on image labels, shared media content, and labelled image categories. Zhong et al. (2016) make use of pixel level image features and report that a combination of those visual features and features derived from captions gives best performance. They also employ these features for predicting which images are *bully-prone*. These are images that are likely to attract hate speech comments, and are referred to as *bullying triggers*.

4 Persons Involved in Bullying Episodes and Their Roles

Apart from detecting hateful messages, a group of works focuses on persons involved in hate speech episodes and their roles. Xu et al. (2012) look at the entire bullying event (or *bullying trace*), automatically assigning roles to actors involved in the event as well as the message author. They differentiate between the roles *bully*, *victim*, *assistant*, *defender*, *bystander*, *reinforcer*, *reporter* and *accuser* for tweet authors and for person mentions within the tweet. Aside from classifying insulting messages, Sood et al. (2012b) also automatically predict whether such messages are directed at an author of a previous comment or at a third party. Silva et al. (2016) provide an analysis of the main hate target groups on the two social media platforms Twitter and Whisper. The authors conclude that both platforms exhibit the same top 6 hate target groups: People are mostly bullied for their ethnicity, behaviour, physical characteristics, sexual orientation, class or gender. Chau and Xu (2007) present a study of a selected set of 28 anti-Black *hate groups* in blogs on the Xanga site. Using a semi-automated approach, they find demographical and topological characteristics of these groups. Using web-link and -content analysis, Zhou et al. (2005) examine the structure of US domestic extremist groups.

5 Anticipating Alarming Societal Changes

Apart from detecting individual, isolated hateful comments and classifying the types of users involved, the overall *proportion* of extreme negative posts over a certain time-span also allows for interesting avenues of research. Insights into changes in public or personal mood can be gained. Information on notable *increases* in the number of hateful posts within a short time span might indicate suspicious developments in a community. Such information could be utilized to circumvent incidents such as racial violence, terrorist attacks, or other crimes before they happen, thus providing steps in the direction of *anticipatory governance*.

One work concerned with crime prediction is Wang et al. (2012). This work focuses on forecasting hit-and-run crimes from Twitter data by effectively employing semantic role labelling and event-based topic extraction (with *LDA*). Burnap et al. (2013) examine the automatic detection of *tension* in social media. They establish that it can be reliably detected and visualized over time using sentiment analysis and lexical resources encoding topic-specific actors, accusations and abusive terms. Williams and Burnap (2015) temporally relate online hate speech with offline terrorist events. They find that the first hours following a terrorist event are the critical time span in which online hate speech may likely occur.

6 Classification Methods

The methods utilized for hate speech detection in terms of classifiers are predominantly supervised learning approaches. As classifiers mostly *Support Vector Machines* are used. Among the more recent methods, deep learning with *Recurrent Neural Network Language Models* has been employed in Mehdad and Tetreault (2016). There

[11]One example documenting disturbing cases of gender-based hate on facebook is `www.womenactionmedia.org/examples-of-gender-based-hate-speech-on- facebook/`

exist no comparative studies which would allow making judgement on the most effective learning method.

The different works also differ in the choice of classification procedure: Standard one-step classification approaches exist along with multi-step classification approaches. The latter approaches employ individual classifiers that solve subproblems, such as establishing negative polarity (§3.3).

Furthermore, some works employ semi-supervised approaches, particularly bootstrapping, which can be utilized for different purposes in the context of hate speech detection. On the one hand, it can be used to obtain additional training data, as it is for example done in Xiang et al. (2012). In this work, first a set of Twitter *users* is divided into *good* and *bad users*, based on the number of offensive terms present in their posts. Then *all* existing tweets of those bad users are selected and added to the training set as hate speech instances.

In addition, bootstrapping can also be utilized to build lexical resources used as part of the detection process. Gitari et al. (2015) apply this method to populate their hate verb lexicon, starting with a small seed verb list, and iteratively expanding it based on WordNet relations, adding all synonyms and hypernyms of those seed verbs.

7 Data and Annotation

To be able to perform experiments on hate speech detection, access to labelled corpora is essential. Since there is no commonly accepted benchmark corpus for the task, authors usually collect and label their own data. The data sources that are used include: Twitter (Xiang et al., 2012; Xu et al., 2012; Burnap et al., 2013; Burnap et al., 2014; Burnap and Williams, 2015; Silva et al., 2016), Instagram (Hosseinmardi et al., 2015; Zhong et al., 2016), Yahoo! (Nobata et al., 2016; Djuric et al., 2015; Warner and Hirschberg, 2012), YouTube (Dinakar et al., 2012), ask.fm (Van Hee et al., 2015), Formspring (Dinakar et al., 2012), Usenet (Razavi et al., 2010), Whisper[12] (Silva et al., 2016), and Xanga[13] (Chau and Xu, 2007). Since these sites have been created for different purposes, they may have special characteristics, and may therefore display different subtypes of hate speech. For instance, on a platform specially created for adolescents, one should expect quite different types of hate speech than on a service that is used by a cross-section of the general public since the resulting different demographics will have an impact on the topics discussed and the language used. These implications should be considered when interpreting the results of research conducted on a particular social media platform.

In general, the size of collected corpora varies considerably in works on hate speech detection, ranging from around 100 labelled comments used in the knowledge-based work by Dinakar et al. (2012) to several thousand comments used in other works, such as Van Hee et al. (2015) or Djuric et al. (2015). Apart from the classification approach taken, another reason for these size differences lies in the simple fact that annotating hate speech is an extremely time consuming endeavour: There are much fewer hateful than benign comments present in randomly sampled data, and therefore a large number of comments have to be annotated to find a considerable number of hate speech instances. This skewed distribution makes it generally difficult and costly to build a corpus that is balanced with respect to hateful and harmless comments. The size of a data set should always be taken into consideration when assessing the effectiveness of certain features or (learning) methods applied on it. Their effectiveness – or lack thereof – may be the result of a particular data size. For instance, features that tackle word generalization (§3.2) are extremely important when dealing with small data sets while on very large data sets they become less important since data sparsity is a less of an issue. We are not aware of any study examining the relation between the size of labeled training data and features/classifiers for hate speech detection.

In order to increase the share of hate speech messages while keeping the size of data instances to be annotated at a reasonable level, Waseem and Hovy (2016)[14] propose to pre-select the text instances to be annotated by querying a site for topics which are likely to contain a higher degree of hate speech (e.g. *Islam terror*). While this increases the proportion of hate speech posts on resulting data sets, it focuses the resulting data set to specific topics and certain subtypes of hate speech (e.g. hate speech targeting Muslims).

In order to annotate a data set manually, either expert annotators are used or crowdsourcing ser-

[12] `http://whisper.sh`

[13] `http://xanga.com`

[14] The data from this work are available under `http://github.com/zeerakw/hatespeech`

vices, such as Amazon Mechanical Turk (AMT), are employed. Crowdsourcing has obvious economical and organizational advantages, especially for a task as time-consuming as the one at hand, but annotation quality might suffer from employing non-expert annotators. Nobata et al. (2016) compare crowdsourced annotations performed using AMT with annotations created by expert annotators and find large differences in agreement.

In addition to the issues mentioned above that, to some extent, challenge the comparability of the research conducted on various data sets, the fact that no commonly accepted definition of hate speech exists further exacerbates this situation.

Previous works remain fairly vague when it comes to the annotation guidelines their annotators were given for their work. Ross et al. (2016) point out that this is particularly a problem for hate speech detection. Despite providing annotators with a definition of hate speech, in their work the annotators still fail to produce an annotation at an acceptable level of reliability.

8 Challenges

As the previous section suggests, the community would considerably benefit from a benchmark data set for the hate speech detection task underlying a commonly accepted definition of the task.

With the exception of Dutch (Van Hee et al., 2015) and German (Ross et al., 2016), we are not aware of any significant research being done on hate speech detection other than on English language data. We think that particularly a multilingual perspective to hate speech may be worthwhile. Unlike other tasks in NLP, hate speech may have strong cultural implications, that is, depending on one's particular cultural background, an utterance may be perceived as offensive or not. It remains to be seen in how far established approaches to hate speech detection examined on English are equally effective on other languages.

Although in the previous sections we also described approaches that try to incorporate the context of hate speech by employing some specific knowledge-based features (§3.6), meta-information (§3.7) or multi-modal information (§3.8), we still feel that there has been comparatively little work looking into these types of features. In the following, we illustrate the necessity of incorporating such context knowledge with the help of three difficult instances of hate speech. For all these cases, it is unclear whether the methods we described in this survey would correctly recognize these remarks as hate speech.

In (6) a woman is ridiculed for her voice. There is no explicit evaluation of her voice but it is an obvious inference from being compared with *Kermit the frog*. In (7), a Muslim is accused of bestiality. Again, there is no explicit accusation. The speaker of that utterance relies on his addressee to be aware of stereotyped prejudices against Islam. Finally, in (8), the speaker of that utterance wants to offend some girls by suggesting they are unattractive. Again, there is no explicit mention of being unattractive but challenging someone else's opposite view can be interpreted in this way.

(6) Kermit the frog called and he wants his voice back.
(7) Your goat is calling.
(8) Who was responsible for convincing these girls they were so pretty?

These examples are admittedly difficult cases and we are not aware of one individual method which would cope with all of these examples. It remains to be seen, whether in the future new computational approaches can actually solve these problems or whether hate speech is a research problem similar to sarcasm where only certain subtypes have been shown to be automatically detected with the help of NLP (Riloff et al., 2013).

9 Conclusion

In this paper, we presented a survey on the automatic detection of hate speech. This task is usually framed as a supervised learning problem. Fairly generic features, such as bag of words or embeddings, systematically yield reasonable classification performance. Character-level approaches work better than token-level approaches. Lexical resources, such as list of slurs, may help classification, but usually only in combination with other types of features. Various complex features using more linguistic knowledge, such as dependency-parse information, or features modelling specific linguistic constructs, such as imperatives or politeness, have also been shown to be effective. Information derived from text may not be the only cue suggesting the presence of hate speech. It may be complemented by meta-information or information from other modalities (e.g. images attached to messages). Making judgements about the general effectiveness of many of the complex features is difficult since, in most cases, they are only evaluated on individual data sets, most of which are not publicly available and often only address a subtype of hate speech, such as bullying of particular ethnic minorities. For better comparability of different features and methods, we argue for a benchmark data set for hate speech detection.

Acknowledgements

We would like David M. Howcroft for proofreading this paper. The authors were partially supported by the German Research Foundation (DFG) under grant WI 4204/2-1 and the Cluster of Excellence Multimodal Computing and Interaction of the German Excellence Initiative.

References

David M. Blei, Andrew Ng, and Michael I. Jordan. 2003. Latent Dirichlet Allocation. *Journal of Machine Learning Research*, 3:993–1022.

Peter F. Brown, Peter V. deSouza, Robert L. Mercer, Vincent J. Della Pietra, and Jenifer C. Lai. 1992. Class-based n-gram models of natural language. *Computational Linguistics*, 18(4):467–479.

P. Burnap and M. Williams. 2014. Hate speech, machine classification and statistical modelling of information flows on twitter: Interpretation and communication for policy decision making. In *Internet, Policy and Politics Conference*, Oxford, United Kingdom.

Pete Burnap and Matthew L. Williams. 2015. Cyber hate speech on twitter: An application of machine classification and statistical modeling for policy and decision making. *Policy & Internet*, 7(2):223–242.

Pete Burnap and Matthew L. Williams. 2016. Us and them: identifying cyber hate on twitter across multiple protected characteristics. *EPJ Data Science*, 5(1):1–15.

Pete Burnap, Omer F. Rana, Nick Avis, Matthew Williams, William Housley, Adam Edwards, Jeffrey Morgan, and Luke Sloan. 2013. Detecting tension in online communities with computational twitter analysis. *Technological Forecasting and Social Change*, pages 96–108, May.

Pete Burnap, Matthew L. Williams, Luke Sloan, Omer Rana, William Housley, Adam Edwards, Vincent Knight, Rob Procter, and Alex Voss. 2014. Tweeting the terror: modelling the social media reaction to the woolwich terrorist attack. *Social Network Analysis and Mining*, 4(1):1–14.

Michael Chau and Jennifer Xu. 2007. Mining communities and their relationships in blogs: A study of online hate groups. *International Journal of Human-Computer Studies*, 65(1):57–70.

Ying Chen, Yilu Zhou, Sencun Zhu, and Heng Xu. 2012. Detecting offensive language in social media to protect adolescent online safety. In *Privacy, Security, Risk and Trust (PASSAT), 2012 International Conference on and 2012 International Conference on Social Computing (SocialCom)*, pages 71–80, Amsterdam, Netherlands, September. IEEE.

Maral Dadvar, Franciska MG de Jong, RJF Ordelman, and RB Trieschnigg. 2012. Improved cyberbullying detection using gender information. *DIR 2012*, pages 22–25.

Maral Dadvar, Dolf Trieschnigg, Roeland Ordelman, and Franciska de Jong. 2013. Improving Cyberbullying Detection with User Context. In *Proceedings of the European Conference in Information Retrieval (ECIR)*, pages 693–696, Moscow, Russia.

Karthik Dinakar, Birago Jones, Catherine Havasi, Henry Lieberman, and Rosalind Picard. 2012. Common sense reasoning for detection, prevention, and mitigation of cyberbullying. *ACM Trans. Interact. Intell. Syst.*, 2(3):18:1–18:30, September.

Nemanja Djuric, Jing Zhou, Robin Morris, Mihajlo Grbovic, Vladan Radosavljevic, and Narayan Bhamidipati. 2015. Hate speech detection with comment embeddings. In *Proceedings of the 24th International Conference on World Wide Web*, pages 29–30, New York, NY, USA. ACM.

Njagi Dennis Gitari, Zhang Zuping, Hanyurwimfura Damien, and Jun Long. 2015. A lexicon-based approach for hate speech detection. *International Journal of Multimedia and Ubiquitous Engineering*, 10(4):215–230.

Homa Hosseinmardi, Sabrina Arredondo Mattson, Rahat Ibn Rafiq, Richard Han, Qin Lv, and Shivakant Mishra. 2015. Detection of cyberbullying incidents on the instagram social network. *CoRR*, abs/1503.03909.

Irene Kwok and Yuzhou Wang. 2013. Locate the hate: Detecting tweets against blacks. In Marie desJardins and Michael L. Littman, editors, *AAAI*, pages 1621–1622, Bellevue, Washington, USA. AAAI Press.

Quoc Le and Tomas Mikolov. 2014. Distributed Representations of Sentences and Documents. In *Proceedings of the International Conference on Machine Learning (JMLR)*, pages 1188–1196, Beijing, China.

Hugo Liu and Push Singh. 2004. ConceptNet: A Practical Commonsense Reasoning Toolkit. *BT Technology Journal*, 22:211–226.

Yashar Mehdad and Joel Tetreault. 2016. Do characters abuse more than words? In *17th Annual Meeting of the Special Interest Group on Discourse and Dialogue*, pages 299–303, Los Angeles, CA, USA.

Tomas Mikolov, Kai Chen, Greg Corrado, and Jeffrey Dean. 2013. Efficient Estimation of Word Representations in Vector Space. In *Proceedings of Workshop at the International Conference on Learning Representations (ICLR)*, Scottsdale, AZ, USA.

Chikashi Nobata, Joel Tetreault, Achint Thomas, Yashar Mehdad, and Yi Chang. 2016. Abusive language detection in online user content. In *Proceedings of the 25th International Conference on World Wide Web*, pages 145–153, Geneva, Switzerland.

John T. Nockleby. 2000. Hate Speech. In Leonard W. Levy, Kenneth L. Karst, and Dennis J. Mahoney, editors, *Encyclopedia of the American Constitution*, pages 1277–1279. Macmillan, 2nd edition.

Amir H. Razavi, Diana Inkpen, Sasha Uritsky, and Stan Matwin. 2010. Offensive language detection using multi-level classification. In *Proceedings of the 23rd Canadian Conference on Advances in Artificial Intelligence*, AI'10, pages 16–27, Berlin, Heidelberg.

Ellen Riloff, Ashequl Qadir, Prafulla Surve, Lalindra De Silva, Nathan Gilbert, and Ruihong Huang. 2013. Sarcasm as Contrast between a Positive Sentiment and Negative Situation. In *Proceedings of the Conference on Empirical Methods in Natural Language Processing (EMNLP)*, pages 704–714, Seattle, WA, USA.

Björn Ross, Michael Rist, Guillermo Carbonell, Benjamin Cabrera, Nils Kurowsky, and Michael Wojatzki. 2016. Measuring the Reliability of Hate Speech Annotations: The Case of the European Refugee Crisis. In *Proceedings of the Workshop on Natural Language Processing for Computer-Mediated Communication (NLP4CMC)*, pages 6–9, Bochum, Germany.

Leandro Araújo Silva, Mainack Mondal, Denzil Correa, Fabrício Benevenuto, and Ingmar Weber. 2016. Analyzing the targets of hate in online social media. In *Proceedings of the Tenth International Conference on Web and Social Media*, pages 687–690, Cologne, Germany.

Sara Sood, Judd Antin, and Elizabeth Churchill. 2012a. Profanity use in online communities. In *Proceedings of the SIGCHI Conference on Human Factors in Computing Systems*, pages 1481–1490, Austin, TX, USA. ACM.

Sara Owsley Sood, Elizabeth F. Churchill, and Judd Antin. 2012b. Automatic identification of personal insults on social news sites. *J. Am. Soc. Inf. Sci. Technol.*, 63(2):270–285, February.

Ellen Spertus. 1997. Smokey: Automatic recognition of hostile messages. In *Proceedings of the Fourteenth National Conference on Artificial Intelligence and Ninth Conference on Innovative Applications of Artificial Intelligence*, AAAI'97/IAAI'97, pages 1058–1065, Providence, RI, USA. AAAI Press.

Mike Thelwall, Kevan Buckley, Georgios Paltoglou, and Di Cai. 2010. Sentiment Strength Detection in Short Informal Text. *Journal of the American Society for Information Science and Technology*, 61(12):2544–2558.

Cynthia Van Hee, Els Lefever, Ben Verhoeven, Julie Mennes, Bart Desmet, Guy De Pauw, Walter Daelemans, and Véronique Hoste. 2015. Detection and fine-grained classification of cyberbullying events. In *Proceedings of Recent Advances in Natural Language Processing, Proceedings*, pages 672–680, Hissar, Bulgaria.

Xiaofeng Wang, Matthew S Gerber, and Donald E Brown. 2012. Automatic crime prediction using events extracted from twitter posts. In *International Conference on Social Computing, Behavioral-Cultural Modeling, and Prediction*, pages 231–238.

William Warner and Julia Hirschberg. 2012. Detecting hate speech on the world wide web. In *Proceedings of the Second Workshop on Language in Social Media*, LSM '12, pages 19–26, Stroudsburg, PA, USA. Association for Computational Linguistics.

Zeerak Waseem and Dirk Hovy. 2016. Hateful symbols or hateful people? predictive features for hate speech detection on twitter. In *Proceedings of the NAACL Student Research Workshop*, pages 88–93, San Diego, California, USA, June. Association for Computational Linguistics.

Matthew Leighton Williams and Pete Burnap. 2015. Cyberhate on social media in the aftermath of woolwich: A case study in computational criminology and big data. *British Journal of Criminology*, pages 211–238.

Guang Xiang, Bin Fan, Ling Wang, Jason Hong, and Carolyn Rose. 2012. Detecting offensive tweets via topical feature discovery over a large scale twitter corpus. In *Proceedings of the 21st ACM international conference on Information and knowledge management*, pages 1980–1984, Maui, HI, USA. ACM.

Jun-Ming Xu, Kwang-Sung Jun, Xiaojin Zhu, and Amy Bellmore. 2012. Learning from bullying traces in social media. In *Proceedings of the 2012 conference of the North American chapter of the association for computational linguistics: Human language technologies*, pages 656–666, Montréal, Canada. Association for Computational Linguistics.

Haoti Zhong, Hao Li, Anna Cinzia Squicciarini, Sarah Michele Rajtmajer, Christopher Griffin, David J. Miller, and Cornelia Caragea. 2016. Content-driven detection of cyberbullying on the instagram social network. In *IJCAI*, pages 3952–3958, New York City, NY, USA. IJCAI/AAAI Press.

Yilu Zhou, Edna Reid, Jialun Qin, Hsinchun Chen, and Guanpi Lai. 2005. US Domestic Extremist Groups on the Web: Link and Content Analysis. *IEEE intelligent systems*, 20(5):44–51.

Facebook Sentiment: Reactions and Emojis

Ye Tian[1], **Thiago Galery**[2,3]
[1]Laboratoire Linguistique Formelle,
Université Paris-Diderot, Paris, France
[2]DBpedia Association
& [3]Idio, London, UK
tiany.03@gmail.com
tgalery@gmail.com

Giulio Dulcinati[4],
Emilia Molimpakis[4] **& Chao Sun**[4]
[4]Division of Psychology
and Language Sciences,
University College London, London, UK
g.dulcinati@gmail.com
emilia.molimpakis@ucl.ac.uk
chao.sun.13@ucl.ac.uk

Abstract

Emojis are used frequently in social media. A widely assumed view is that emojis express the emotional state of the user, which has led to research focusing on the expressiveness of emojis independent from the linguistic context. We argue that emojis and the linguistic texts can modify the meaning of each other. The overall communicated meaning is not a simple sum of the two channels. In order to study the meaning interplay, we need data indicating the overall sentiment of the entire message as well as the sentiment of the emojis stand-alone. We propose that Facebook Reactions are a good data source for such a purpose. FB reactions (e.g. "Love" and "Angry") indicate the readers' overall sentiment, against which we can investigate the types of emojis used the comments under different reaction profiles. We present a data set of 21,000 FB posts (57 million reactions and 8 million comments) from public media pages across four countries.

1 Introduction

We use social media not only to share information, but also to express emotions. This paper presents a data set of multi-cultural Facebook (FB) posts from public media pages, the readers' reactions and the emojis contained in the comments. We argue that this data set - one that can be up-scaled in size, in genres, and in languages/cultures - is a useful and cheap resource for investigating the types of emojis used in different emotional contexts.

2 Emojis and Sentiment - Some background

Emoticons, such as ";)", are representations of facial expressions using punctuation symbols. They were first used by the computer scientist Scott Fahlman in 1982 as a "joke marker" (Fahlman, 2012). Recently, emoticons have been gradually replaced by emojis, which are graphic symbols representing facial expressions (e.g. smiling), gestures (e.g. thumbs up), objects (e.g. vehicles) and even actions (e.g. dancing). They have gained popularity rapidly in smartphone texts, emails and social media. On certain platforms (e.g. Instagram), in some countries (e.g. Finland and France), over half of all online messages contain emojis, and this trend is going up worldwide (Dimson, 2015).

Emojis have attracted an increasing amount of research interest in sociology and in computer science. Sociological research is interested in how people with different demographic profiles (age, gender and culture) use emoticons and emojis, how it affects people's relationships and and how it fits the cultural contexts (Huffaker and Calvert, 2005; Sugiyama, 2015; Wolf, 2000; Kelly and Watts, 2015). Research in computer science has primarily focused on using emoticons and emojis as a cue for automatically analysing the sentiment of short messages, commonly tweets (Hu et al., 2013; Novak et al., 2015; Thelwall et al., 2010; Boia et al., 2013; Zhao et al., 2012; Hogenboom et al., 2013). It was found that positive emoticons and emojis are used more frequently than negative ones (Novak et al., 2015). The polarity of emoticons and emojis is relatively well correlated with the perceived emotional polarity of the entire text, but is poorly correlated with the perceived emotional polarity of the accompanying linguistic text alone (Boia et al., 2013). Using emoticons and

Proceedings of the Fifth International Workshop on Natural Language Processing for Social Media , pages 11–16,
Valencia, Spain, April 3-7, 2017. ©2017 Association for Computational Linguistics

emojis as a cue for sentiment analysis of tweets results in better accuracy compared to using the linguistic text alone (Hogenboom et al., 2013; Hu et al., 2013; Zhao et al., 2012), to a level between 60% to 75%. Emojis tend to be a better indicator for an overall negative tweet than a positive one.

Although the polarity of emojis frequently mismatch the polarity of the accompanying linguistic text or even the entire message, little has been done to analyze the nature of these mismatches. The default assumption is that emojis express the user's emotional state, therefore they can be seen as an independent channel of communication from that of the linguistic text. For example, (Novak et al., 2015) offered sentiment scores for 751 most frequently used emojis, calculated using the sentiment rating of 1.6 million tweets in 13 European languages containing these emojis. This significant piece of work has provided a lot of information on the cross-linguistic usage of emojis in tweets. However, treating the average sentiment of tweets containing emojis as the sentiment score of the emojis themselves relies on the assumption that the meaning of emojis are consistent across linguistic contexts.

We argue that emojis and the linguistic text can modify the meaning of each other. The overall communicated meaning is not a simple sum of the two channels. A similar view has been voiced by some linguists. (Baron, 2009) points out that just like linguistic words, the meaning of emoticons and emojis are often under-specified. (Dresner and Herring, 2010) argues against the idea that emoticons are signs of emotion. Drawing on speech act theory, they argue that emoticons are indicators of the illocutionary force of the textual utterance that they accompany. They "neither contribute to the propositional content (the locution) of the language used, nor are they just an extralinguistic communication channel indicating emotion" (Dresner and Herring, 2010) [pp. 255].

We propose that an emoji can interact with the linguistic text in six ways. An emoji can

1. replace a word/phrase.
   e.g. *I want have a* .

2. repeat a word/phrase (accenting, adding focus)
   e.g. *Take note Sam, this is how you season food, you are almost done there babe. Like you did the chicken the other nights.*

3. express the speaker's emotion or attitude independently.
   e.g. *(Facebook update from survivor of the Florida gay club shooting 2016-06-12): I am safely home and hoping everyone gets home safely as well.*

4. enhance/ emphasize an emotion expressed in the text.
   e.g. *This would probably be really good* .

5. modify the meaning of linguistic text (e.g. marking non-literal or non-serious use); implying propositional content
   e.g. *I bet you are enjoying your revision* .

   -A: Would you like to come to my party? -B:

6. be used for politeness.
   e.g. *Can you please cook us something that I tag you in instead of your 4am pastas? Thanks.*

We hypothesize that compared to negative emojis, positive emojis are more often used not as direct reflection of emojis, but are used (1) ironically in a negative context, or (2) for politeness reasons (e.g. in a request or disagreement). These uses are also seen in smiles and laughter in natural dialogue (Mazzocconi et al., 2016). In face-to-face conversations, we may produce an ironic laughter to communicate that an attempted joke was not funny, or smile when we ask for a favour.

In order to study the meaning interplay between linguistic texts and emojis, we need to model contexts where the sentiment of the emojis are consistent with the overall sentiment of the texts, as well as contexts where they are inconsistent. Obtaining such data would normally require a large amount of manual labeling. Instead, we propose that we can cheaply obtain data set for this purposes by looking at Facebook Reactions and emojis in comments.

3 Facebook reactions

Facebook reactions, released in February 2016, are an extension of the old "Like" button. Its six options (Like, Love, Haha, Wow, Sad and Angry) are represented by slightly edited versions of several long-established Unicode Emojis, and they allow for a more nuanced expression of how users feel towards a post. The emotions underlying these six reactions are supposed to be frequent and universal. If we assume that Facebook reactions reflect the readers' overall sentiment towards a post, we can investigate the distributions of emojis in readers' comments, under different emotional attitudes. Thus, if there is a mismatch in the emotional polarity between the overall profile of reactions (e.g. dominantly "Angry" - negative) and the sentiment of the emojis in the comments (e.g. "thumbs up" - positive), these emojis are likely used not to directly reflect emotions.

4 Current data set and analysis

We collected data from 21,000 posts in August 2016 on public media Facebook pages from four countries: UK (bbc, the Daily Mail, Daily Mirror, the Telegraph), US (CNN, Fox News, New York Times, Wall Street Journal, MSNBC), France (Le Figaro, Le Monde, Liberation) and Germany (Die WELT, Frankfurter Allgemeine Zeitung, Suddeutsche Zeitung). These posts were shared 15,273,365 times. There were 57,444,404 reactions and 8,463,602 comments to these posts. We tried to balance the political leanings of the selected media. The purpose of analyzing data from different countries was to see whether the way we use Facebook Reactions and emojis can be generalized cross-culturally/linguistically. We analyzed the reactions, sharing behaviours, and the emojis that appeared in the comments. The data set contains country, name of media, the title of the posts, the link to the full article (if any), the time of posting, the total times shared, the total number of reactions, a breakdown of reactions (Likes, Loves, etc), the total number of comments, and the texts of the comments[1].

5 Results - Facebook Reactions

In terms of reactions (figure1), we found that "Like", being the default reaction, is unsurprisingly the most frequent (overall 78.9%). The frequency of the other fie reactions ranks as "Love" (5.5%), "Angry" (5.4%) "Sad" (4.0%), "Haha" (3.7%), "Wow" (2.5%).

There are small but statistically different differences cross countries ($p < 2.2e\text{-}16$). "Angry' is the most frequent in France at 9% and the least frequent in the UK at 3%. "Love" is the highest in the

[1] As of 23/02/2017, the authors are still discussing with Facebook regarding the details of data release options.

Figure 1: Facebook Reactions distribution (the small pie shows the zoomed-in distribution of reactions other than "Like")

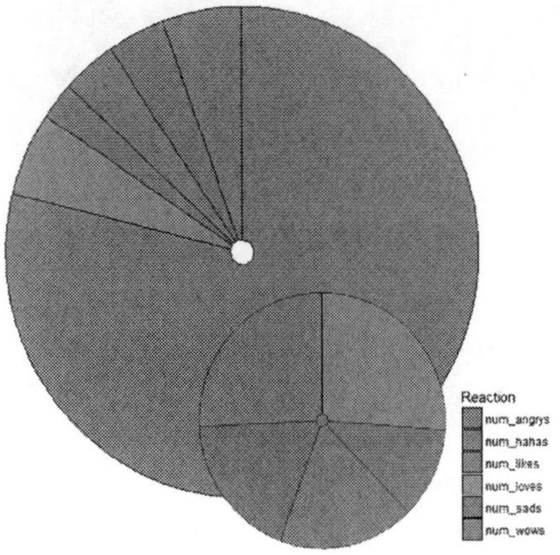

US at 6% and lowest in Germany at 2%. "Haha" is the highest in Germany at 6% and lowest in the UK at 3%. The overall comments to reaction ratio is 0.15, and sharing to reaction ratio is 0.27.

We calculated the proportions of each of the six Reactions for all posts (for example, a post could have 80% "Like", 10% "Wow", 5% "Haha", 5% "Love", and 0% of "Angry" or "Sad"), and applied K-means clustering algorithm to these Reaction proportions. We found four major profiles of Reactions (figure 2), which we label "Just likes", "Amused/Surprised", "Angry" and "Sad". The first cluster is characterized by almost all reactions being "Like". The second cluster has a significant percentage of "Haha"s but also some "Angry"s. In both the "Angry" and "Sad" clusters, less than half of the reactions are "Like"s. In the "Angry" cluster, 41% of reactions are "Angry" and 8% are "Sad". In "Sad" cluster, 40% of reactions are "Sad" while 9% are "Angry". We calculated the Share to Reaction ratios (number of Shares/ number of Reactions), and found them to be different in different Reaction profiles: 0.16 for "Just likes", 0.24 for "Amused/Surprised", 0.33 for "Angry" and 0.24 for "Sad": people are more likely to share a post when the reaction is something other than "Like", suggesting that stronger emotional attitude leads to more post sharing.

5.1 Results - Emojis

We randomly sampled 100,000 emoji-containing comments, and processed the emojis by matching them against a dictionary of emoji Unicode.

Figure 2: Four profiles of FB Reactions

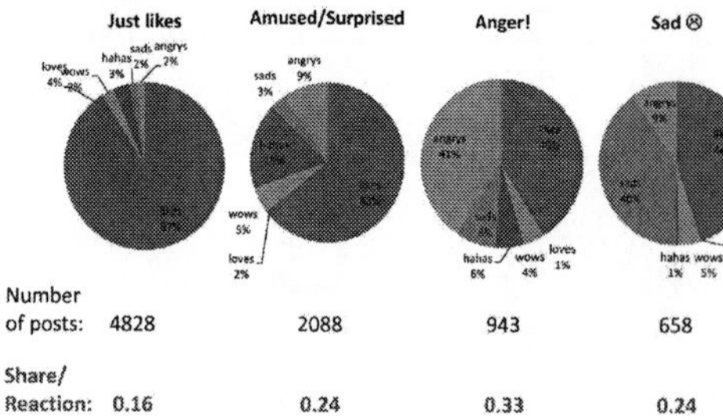

These emojis can then be more easily counted and be matched with the emoji sentiment score from (Novak et al., 2015). We found that in our data, the most frequent emojis are “thumbs up”, “face with heart shaped eyes”, “claps”, “angry face” and “winking face” (Figure 3). This is different from that of Twitter emoji distribution based on http://www.emojitracker.com/, where the most frequent is “face with tears of joy”. We cannot generalize this to a difference between Facebook and Twitter emoji use. Our data, being being comments to news articles on public pages, are likely less personal and more evaluative, and hence the frequent uses of “thumbs up”. Unlike words in natural language, emoji frequencies do not seem to follow a Zipfian distribution, leading to a hypothesis that the senses of emojis overlap more than that of linguistic words. We found that positive emojis are more frequent than negative ones, which is consistent with previous findings (Novak et al., 2015).

Figure 3: Emoji frequencies in FB comments on media pages

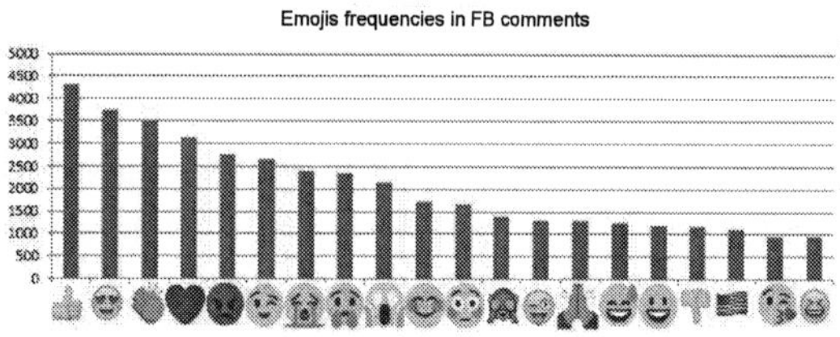

We found that emoji distributions vary across countries (figure 4). All countries use positive emojis more frequently than negative ones. France uses “angry face” frequently, consistent with the fact that the “Angry” reaction is the most frequent in France among the four countries. Both the UK and the US use “crying face”/ “face with tears” frequently. The US also frequently uses the “American flag” emoji, though this may be due

Figure 4: FB Emoji distribution by country

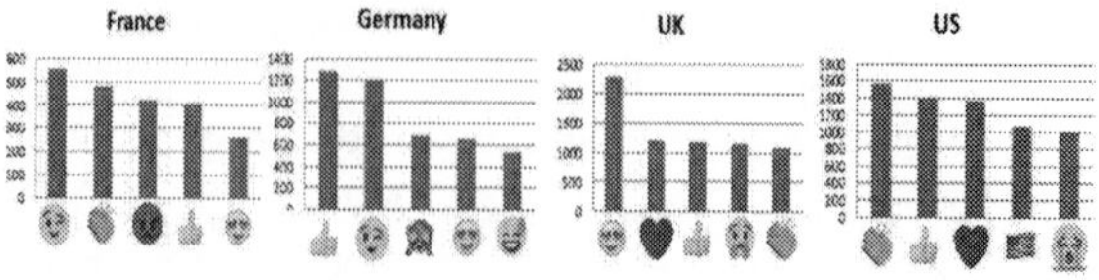

to the data been collected during the US election campaign (August 2016).

Emoji distributions are different in different Reaction profiles (figure 5). The most frequent emojis under “Just likes” are all positive. Under “Amused/Surprised” there are a mixture of positive emojis (e.g. “thumbs up”) and negative/neutral emojis (e.g. “astonished face”) indicating surprise. Interestingly, while the most frequent emojis under “Sad” all have negative sentiment, a significant amount of emojis under Angry are positive (e.g. thumbs up and clapping hands). This suggests that users often use emojis ironically when their overall attitude is Angry.

Using the sentiment scores compiled for emojis by (Novak et al., 2015), we calculated the average emoji-based sentiment score for each comment containing emojis. We assumed that repetitions of emojis likely express a stronger sentiment than a single use, but the marginal increase of each repetition should gradually diminish, i.e., the use of three “heart shapes” in a row express a stronger sentiment than one “heart shape”, but not three times as much. Taking this into account, we calculated the emoji-based sentiment of comments using:

$$\frac{1}{n}\sum_{i=1}^{n} log((number\ of\ emoji_i)+1)\times sentiment\ of\ emoji_i$$

$$n = the\ total\ number\ of\ distinct\ emojis$$

For example, if a comment contains three “faces with tears of joy” and one “winking face”, the emoji-based sentiment of the comment would be calculated as ((log(3)+1)*0.22 + (log(1)+1)*0.46)/2 = 0.46. Then, we calculated the emoji-based sentiment score of each post by averaging the emoji-based sentiment scores of all comments for this post. The scores for the four Reaction profiles of posts are: 0.41 for "Just likes", 0.34 for "Amused/Surprised", 0.24 for "Angry" and 0.24 for "Sad". Though the scores for the first two profiles are higher (and therefore more positive) than the last two, the difference is small, and the sentiment scores for "Angry" and "Sad" are still positive when negative values should be expected. We think two factors may have dampened the difference between scores of the positive profiles and the negative profiles. First, like we mentioned before, the emoji sentiment scores from (Novak et al., 2015) were calculated from the sentiment of entire tweets. If positive emojis are sometimes used in negative contexts (ironically or for politeness), this method would render lower scores of *positive* emojis than what what would have been the scores when they are used "literally" (directly reflect emotions). Second, we saw that positive emojis are often used in overall negative profiles, e.g. "clapping hands" are frequently used in the "Angry" Reaction profile. These are contexts where many of the emojis are used ironically, or are used for marking that the accompanying text is ironic. Therefore, using the sentiment scores of these positive emojis to calculate the sentiment of the entire comments will lead to misleading results. This further demonstrates the fact that emojis and linguistic texts can modify the meaning of each other, and it is important to study how the meaning interplay works.

Figure 5: FB Emoji distribution by Reaction profile

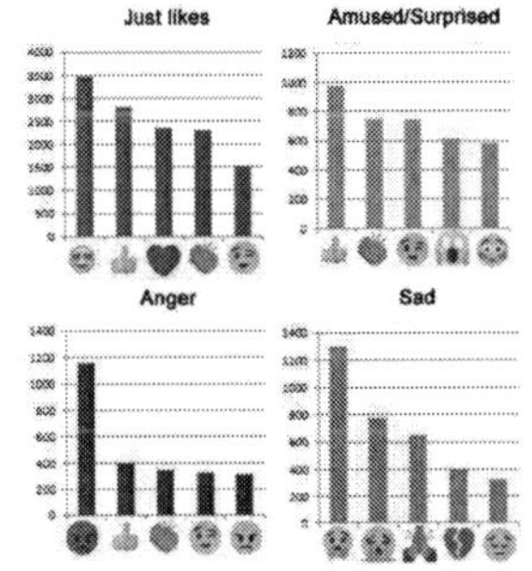

6 Future studies

Our next step is to model contexts of emojis, distinguishing those where emojis directly reflect emotions, and those where the meaning of emojis are modified. In addition, to know whether any of the the cross-country differences we found are indeed due to cultural factors rather than due to the major events happening in each country, we need to obtain data over a longer period of time from a wider varieties of FB pages.

7 Conclusions

Our results show that there is a reliable correlation between Facebook reactions and emoji usages, suggesting that emojis *can* be used to detect users sentiment, if we take into account of contexts where their meanings are modified (used ironically or for politeness). This study also demonstrates that Facebook reactions and comments are a good data source for investigating indicators of user emotional attitudes.

References

Naomi Baron. 2009. The myth of impoverished signal: Dispelling the spoken-language fallacy for emoticons in online communication. In Jane Vincent and Leopoldina Fortunati, editors, *Electronic emotions: The mediation of emotion via information and comunication technologies*, pages 107–135. Peter Lang, Oxford.

Marina Boia, Boi Faltings, Claudiu-Cristian Musat, and Pearl Pu. 2013. A:) is worth a thousand words: How people attach sentiment to emoticons and words in tweets. In *Social Computing (SocialCom), 2013 International Conference on*, pages 345–350. IEEE.

Thomas Dimson. 2015. Emojineering: Machine learning for emoji trends by instagram. http://instagram-engineering.tumblr.com/post/117889701472/emojineering-part-1-machine-learning-for-emoji. Accessed: 2016-06-12.

Eli Dresner and Susan C. Herring. 2010. Functions of the nonverbal in cmc: Emoticons and illocutionary force. *Communication theory*, 20(3):249–268.

Scott E. Fahlman. 2012. Smiley lore:-. *Scott E. Fahlmans Homepage*.

Alexander Hogenboom, Daniella Bal, Flavius Frasincar, Malissa Bal, Franciska de Jong, and Uzay Kaymak. 2013. Exploiting emoticons in sentiment analysis. In *Proceedings of the 28th Annual ACM Symposium on Applied Computing*, pages 703–710. ACM.

Xia Hu, Jiliang Tang, Huiji Gao, and Huan Liu. 2013. Unsupervised sentiment analysis with emotional signals. In *Proceedings of the 22nd international conference on World Wide Web*, pages 607–618. International World Wide Web Conferences Steering Committee.

David A. Huffaker and Sandra L. Calvert. 2005. Gender, identity, and language use in teenage blogs. *Journal of Computer-Mediated Communication*, 10(2):00–00.

Ryan Kelly and Leon Watts. 2015. Characterising the inventive appropriation of emoji as relationally meaningful in mediated close personal relationships. *Experiences of Technology Appropriation: Unanticipated Users, Usage, Circumstances, and Design.*

Chiara Mazzocconi, Ye Tian, and Jonathan Ginzburg. 2016. Towards a multi-layered analysis of laughter. In *Proceedings of JerSem, the 19th Workshop on the Semantics and Pragmatics of Dialogue.*

Petra Kralj Novak, Jasmina Smailović, Borut Sluban, and Igor Mozetič. 2015. Sentiment of emojis. *PloS one*, 10(12):e0144296.

Satomi Sugiyama. 2015. Kawaii meiru and maroyaka neko: Mobile emoji for relationship maintenance and aesthetic expressions among japanese teens. *First Monday*, 20(10).

Mike Thelwall, Kevan Buckley, Georgios Paltoglou, Di Cai, and Arvid Kappas. 2010. Sentiment strength detection in short informal text. *Journal of the American Society for Information Science and Technology*, 61(12):2544–2558.

Alecia Wolf. 2000. Emotional expression online: Gender differences in emoticon use. *CyberPsychology & Behavior*, 3(5):827–833.

Jichang Zhao, Li Dong, Junjie Wu, and Ke Xu. 2012. Moodlens: an emoticon-based sentiment analysis system for chinese tweets. In *Proceedings of the 18th ACM SIGKDD international conference on Knowledge discovery and data mining*, pages 1528–1531. ACM.

Potential and Limitations of Cross-Domain Sentiment Classification

Dirk von Grünigen
Zurich University of Applied Sciences
vongrdir@zhaw.ch

Martin Weilenmann
Zurich University of Applied Sciences
weilemar@zhaw.ch

Jan Deriu
Zurich University of Applied Sciences
deri@zhaw.ch

Mark Cieliebak
Zurich University of Applied Sciences
ciel@zhaw.ch

Abstract

In this paper we investigate the cross-domain performance of sentiment analysis systems. For this purpose we train a convolutional neural network (CNN) on data from different domains and evaluate its performance on other domains. Furthermore, we evaluate the usefulness of combining a large amount of different smaller annotated corpora to a large corpus. Our results show that more sophisticated approaches are required to train a system that works equally well on various domains.

1 Introduction

Most work regarding sentiment analysis focuses on training and testing a sentiment classifier on data of the same domain. For example a new classifier is trained on tweets and tested on tweets. However, in real-world scenarios the data might originate from different sources and domains. Often it is the case that sentiment analysis is performed on a domain for which there is no training data available. Instead of investing large amounts of money to create such a corpus it would make more sense to use an existing classifier. However, it is not always clear how well the existing classifier generalizes on the target domain. Although, it is obvious that the performance will be affected negatively, the magnitude is not known. This missing information is often useful for assessing the need of generating a new classifier for a given domain which is very costly.

Thus, our work is driven by the question of how useful sentiment classifiers are if we evaluate them with datasets from unseen domains, and if a combination of data from different domains might help to overcome the recurring problem of having too little data.

Furthermore, we assess the usefulness of large weakly supervised corpora where the labels are inferred from properties of the text, e.g. the smileys in the text or the rating of a review. We answer the question of how much gain one can expect from leveraging such corpora.

Usually, cross-domain sentiment analysis has a low performance due to the vocabulary mismatch (Pan et al., 2010). Thus, we asses the impact of word embeddings trained on large amounts of data, thus guaranteeing a large coverage of the vocabulary. We then asses how word embeddings trained on different types of data (e.g. News, Twitter) impact the performance of the system. For this, we train a convolutional neural network (CNN) based on (Deriu et al., 2016) on data from different combinations of domains and evaluate its performance on foreign domains.

Related Work Some research has been done already in the field of cross-domain sentiment classification. Most of the work in this area focuses on the mismatch in the vocabularies of the different domains.

(Pan et al., 2010) overcome the challenge of vocabulary-mismatch by employing a spectral feature alignment algorithm to map domain-specific words to a unified representation which can then be used in conjunction with the domain-independent words to lower the mismatch between the domains. (Blitzer et al., 2007) use structural correspondence learning to adapt the vocabulary of the various domains. (Li et al., 2008) experiment with ensembles of classifiers where each classifier was trained on a specific domain and then used in combination to boost the cross-domain performance. (Bollegala et al., 2011) use a semi-supervised algorithm, which leverages supervised and unsupervised data, to create a sentiment-sensitive thesaurus which is used to

Proceedings of the Fifth International Workshop on Natural Language Processing for Social Media , pages 17–24,
Valencia, Spain, April 3-7, 2017. ©2017 Association for Computational Linguistics

compute the relatedness of words from different domains. (Bollegala et al., 2016) uses the aforementioned sentiment-sensitive thesaurus to generate sentiment-sensitive word embeddings. (Glorot et al., 2011) apply unsupervised cross-domain sentiment classification, where they use spectral embeddings to project words and documents into a low dimensional embedding space. (Yu et al., 2016) borrow ideas from SCL and combine it with auxiliary binary predicition tasks to learn dense sentence embeddings which incorporate sentiment and can be used in a cross-domain context.

Contribution Our work presents an in-depth analysis on the generalization power of the current state-of-the-art in a cross-domain setting. This work can be used to estimate and predict the expected drop in performance for a given sentiment classifier.

2 Experimental Setup

2.1 Training

Model We use a state-of-the-art model based on the CNN used by (Deriu et al., 2016). The architecture is composed by two consecutive convolutional- and pooling-layers followed by a fully-connected and a softmax layer. Table 1 gives an overview on the hyper-parameters used for the CNN.

Hyper-Parameter	Value
Number of convolutional Filters	200
Filter width (both layers)	6
Pooling Length (first layer)	4
Pooling Stride (first layer)	2
Activation	*relu*

Table 1: *Overview of the hyper-parameters chosen for the CNN. Note that we define a layer as one convolutional layer followed by one pooling-layer. For the second pooling layer the length is chosen over the whole feature.*

3-Phase Learning We apply the 3-Phase learning procedure (see Figure 1) proposed by (Severyn et al., 2015) where we first create word embeddings based on the skip-gram model (Mikolov et al., 2013). For our purposes we create embeddings with 52 dimensions as in (Deriu et al., 2016) . In a second step we apply a distant-phase where we pre-train the CNN on a large corpus of weakly su-

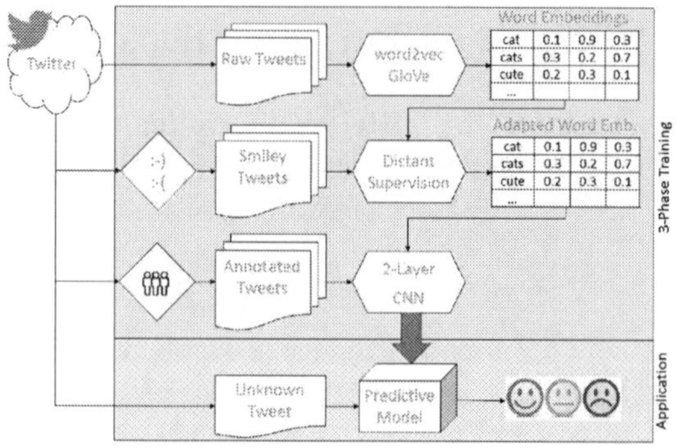

Figure 1: *Overview of the 3-Phase training procedure.*

pervised data, where the sentiment labels are inferred by properties of the texts. In this phase the word embeddings are updated to incorporate sentiment-specific information. The third and final phase is the supervised phase, where we train the CNN on a corpus of manually annotated texts.

Training For the distant-supervised and the supervised phase we employ the *AdaDelta* optimizer to train the CNN. The hyper-parameters are set to the default values of $\epsilon = 1e^{-6}$, $\rho = 0.95$, and the learning rate is set to $lr = 1.0$. Many of the datasets are unbalanced (see Table 2) and, to mitigate this problem, we use class-weights during the learning procedure. The following formula was used to compute the class-weights for each dataset D and each class $i \in S$:

$$c_i = \frac{|D|}{|S| * d_i} \tag{1}$$

where d_i denotes the number of elements in D that belong to class i. Thus, over-represented classes will get a lower weight than under-represented classes. The loss function is scaled with the class-weight for the respective class when training the model.

2.2 Data

For each of the aforementioned phases we experiment with different corpora. We use 3 different corpora for word embeddings, 2 corpora for the distant-supervised phase where the sentiment is inferred by the smiley in case of the tweets and the user ratings in case of the product reviews, and 8 corpora for the supervised phase. A detailed overview of the data is provided in Table 2.

Phase	Dataset	Total	Neutral	Neg.	Pos.	Source
Word Embeddings	Twitter	590M	-	-	-	Public Twitter-API[1]
	News	90M	-	-	-	STATMT website[2]
	Wikipedia	4.5M	-	-	-	Wikimedia[3]
Distant Phase	Reviews	82M	7M	11M	64M	(McAuley et al., 2015)
	Twitter	100M	-	20M	80M	Public Twitter-API[2]
Supervised Phase (Train)	DAI (Tweets)	3274	2191	447	636	(Narr et al., 2012)
	SEval (Tweets)	8226	3958	1210	3058	(Nakov et al., 2016)
	DIL (Reviews)	3420	1739	615	1066	(Ding et al., 2008)
	HUL (Reviews)	3156	1822	438	896	(Hu et al., 2004)
	TAC (Reviews)	2152	381	991	780	(Täckström et al., 2011)
	MPQ (News)	8888	4934	2637	1317	(Wiebe et al., 2005)
	JCR (Quotations)	1032	736	141	155	(Balahur et al., 2013)
	SEM (Headlines)	1000	610	246	144	(Strapparava et al., 2007)
Supervised Phase (Test)	DAI (Tweets)	819	556	101	162	(Narr et al., 2012)
	SEval (Tweets)	3813	1640	601	1572	(Nakov et al., 2016)
	DIL (Reviews)	855	441	144	270	(Ding et al., 2008)
	HUL (Reviews)	789	421	197	171	(Hu et al., 2004)
	TAC (Reviews)	537	65	329	143	(Täckström et al., 2011)
	MPQ (News)	2223	1225	708	290	(Wiebe et al., 2005)
	JCR (Quotations)	258	127	93	38	(Balahur et al., 2013)
	SEM (Headlines)	250	154	66	30	(Strapparava et al., 2007)

Table 2: *Data used for training the CNN model.*

[1] https://dev.twitter.com/rest/public
[2] http://www.statmt.org/wmt14/training-monolingual-news-crawl
[3] https://dumps.wikimedia.org/enwiki/latest/

Evaluation For the evaluation we use the macro-averaged F1-score of positive and negative classes F1 = ($F1_{pos}$ + $F1_{neg}$) / 2, since it is also used in SemEval (Nakov et al., 2016) as standard measure of quality.

3 Experiments & Results

In the following we refer to the system trained on a single target domain (TD) data as *specialized TD system*, a system trained on one foreign domain (FD) dataset and evaluated on the TD test set is called a *specialized FD system*, a system trained on a combinations of FD corpora is called a *generalized FD system*, and a system trained on all data is called a *generalized system*.

3.1 Word Embeddings and Distant-Phase

We train the CNN with all possible combinations of word-embeddings and distant-phases to assess which combination works best for each domain. Additionally we include experiments where we use randomly initialized word embeddings denoted as *Random*, as well as experiments where the distant-phase is omitted, denoted as *None*. Tables 4, 5, and 6 give an overview of the results. In the following we present the main findings.

The complexity among the domains varies. The differences of the averaged scores over each domain are very high. The average score of the *DAI*-tweets is 66 points in F1 score, whereas the average score of the *JCR*-quotations is only at 39.3 points. These differences could be caused by the different sized of the corpora, variations in the quality of the annotations or by the difficulty of the domains itself.

Random word embeddings are not necessarily bad. Generally it is assumed that using pre-trained word embeddings would increase the performance compared to using randomly initialized values. Indeed, the average performance of the random word embeddings (see Table 5.B) lies 3 point below the averages achieved by the *News*-embeddings. Random word embeddings yield the best score only for one domain out of eight. However a closer look at the averaged scores over the combinations of word embeddings and distant-phases (see Table 6) reveals that the combination of random word embeddings with a distant-phase on reviews achieves an average score of 59.4, which is the second-highest average score. Thus, a distant-phase can compensate the lack of pre-trained word embeddings.

Pretrained word embeddings are not necessarily good. The same analysis as above reveals a similar picture for the *Wikipedia*-embeddings. The average score achieved using the *Wikipedia*-embeddings lies 2 points below the average score achieved by the *News*-embeddings. The average scores achieved by using the *Wikipedia*-embeddings on each domain (see Table 5.B) is up to 6 points worse than the best score for the particular domain. Thus, pre-trained word embeddings do not imply an increase in score.

Vocabulary coverage is important. Table 3 shows for each domain the percentage of missing words in the corresponding word embedding. Both the News and Twitter embeddings cover most of the vocabulary. They are missing only up to 3.87% of the vocabulary most of the dataset are missing less than 1% of the vocabulary. On the other hand the Wikipedia embeddings have a much lower coverage, for all of the datasets between 15% and 30% of the vocabulary is not covered. As we have previously seen the *Wikipedia*-embeddings perform worse than the embeddings based on news and tweets. Thus, having an adequate coverage of the vocabulary is important.

	News	Twitter	Wikipedia
DAI	3.87%	3.70%	29.5%
DIL	0.98%	0.85%	21.3%
HUL	1.41%	0.85%	21.9%
JCR	0.31%	1.37%	14.5%
MPQ	0.56%	1.67%	16.9%
SEM	0.53%	1.48%	14.3%
SEval	2.38%	3.01%	26.5%
TAC	1.01%	1.26%	21.2%

Table 3: *Overview of the percentage of missing vocabulary in the word embeddings.*

Distant-Phase as score-booster. Performing a distant-phase yields the best scores for eight out of nine domains, the exception being the *MPQ*-reviews. The average scores achieved performing a distant-phase show the same picture (see Table 5.C *Avg.*-column), where using the *Review*-corpus performs 7 points above omitting the distant-phase. Using tweets for the distant-phase improves the score by 4 points on average. Thus, a distant-phase boosts the performance of the system. This is consistent with the results shown in (Deriu et al., 2016). However we cannot give any recommendation as to which corpus to use, even if using reviews mostly performed better in our case.

	None	Reviews	Twitter
Random	0.502	0.594	0.550
News	0.560	0.604	0.568
Twitter	0.539	0.594	0.585
Wikipedia	0.513	0.586	0.557

Table 6: *Shows the average F1 score for each combination of word embeddings, distant-phase corpus.*

3.2 Cross-Domain Experiments

We train the system on the data of one domain called *target domain* (TD) and test it on the TD as well as the *foreign domains* (FD). The system is optimized for the TD by using the test set of the TD to perform early-stopping. Furthermore we trained the system on the union of all domains and tested it on all the domains separately. For optimization we used the TD test set for early-stopping. For each domain we use the best combination of word embeddings and distant-phase from Section 3.1 as base model (see Table 7). In Table 8 an overview of the results is given.

	Word Emb.	Dist. Phase
DAI	Twitter	Twitter
DIL	Twitter	Reviews
HUL	Wikipedia	Reviews
JCR	Wikipedia	Reviews
MPQ	News	None
SEM	Twitter	Twitter
SEval	News	Twitter
TAC	Random	Reviews

Table 7: *Shows for each domain the best combination of word embeddings and distant phase.*

The generalization power of a specialized systems is poor. As expected the best score is achieved by training and testing on the same domain. However there is a large deterioration in score when the system is tested on another domain than it is trained on. The average score achieved by a specialized FD system on the TD is far below the scores achieved for a specialized TD system. The differences range from 15 (*JCR*) up to 30 (*DAI* and *DIL*) points in F1 score.

Embedding Type	DAI (T/ 3.2k)	MPQ (N/ 8.8k)	DIL (R/ 3.4k)	TAC (R/ 2.1k)	SEM (H/ 3.1k)	JCR (Q/ 1k)	SEval (T/ 8.2k)	HUL (R/ 3.1k)	Union
Random	0.599	0.469	**0.509**	0.577	0.436	0.263	0.598	**0.513**	0.550
News	**0.631**	**0.581**	0.485	**0.644**	0.527	**0.405**	**0.673**	0.480	**0.615**
Twitter	0.629	0.504	0.507	0.585	**0.541**	0.360	0.629	0.511	0.584
Wikipedia	0.553	0.529	0.455	0.570	*0.506*	0.375	0.613	0.451	0.567
Average	0.603	0.520	0.489	0.594	0.502	0.351	0.628	0.489	0.579

(a) No Distant Phase

Embedding Type	DAI (T/ 3.2k)	MPQ (N/ 8.8k)	DIL (R/ 3.4k)	TAC (R/ 2.1k)	SEM (H/ 3.1k)	JCR (Q/ 1k)	SEval (T/ 8.2k)	HUL (R/ 3.1k)	Union
Random	0.698	0.539	0.595	**0.714**	0.477	0.401	0.659	0.659	0.603
News	0.692	**0.563**	0.590	0.682	**0.519**	0.433	**0.685**	0.649	**0.624**
Twitter	**0.701**	0.540	**0.603**	0.694	0.472	0.383	0.683	0.657	0.611
Wikipedia	0.661	0.542	0.569	0.684	0.500	**0.457**	0.622	**0.666**	0.577
Average	0.688	0.546	0.589	0.694	0.492	0.418	0.662	0.658	0.604

(b) Review Distant Phase

Embedding Type	DAI (T/ 3.2k)	MPQ (N/ 8.8k)	DIL (R/ 3.4k)	TAC (R/ 2.1k)	SEM (H/ 3.1k)	JCR (Q/ 1k)	SEval (T/ 8.2k)	HUL (R/ 3.1k)	Union
Random	0.684	0.490	0.523	0.612	0.468	0.399	0.659	0.517	0.595
News	0.678	**0.567**	**0.546**	**0.676**	0.539	0.412	**0.691**	**0.554**	0.444
Twitter	**0.734**	0.518	0.543	0.652	**0.554**	**0.412**	0.685	0.553	**0.610**
Wikipedia	0.663	0.544	0.520	0.619	0.505	0.411	0.642	0.531	0.580
Average	0.690	0.530	0.533	0.640	0.517	0.409	0.669	0.539	0.558

(c) Twitter Distant Phase

Table 4: *Shows the score for each combination of word embeddings, distant-phase corpus, and domain. The last row shows the average score achieved on a particular dataset. The scores in bold denote the best score achieved on the dataset. For each domain we denote the text-type as follows: T: Tweets, N: News, R: Reviews, H: Headlines and Q: Quotations. Alongside with the text-type we also note the size of the corpus.*

	DAI	MPQ	DIL	TAC	SEM	JCR	SEval	HUL	Union
Full Average	0.660	0.532	0.537	0.643	0.504	0.393	0.653	0.562	0.580

(a) Shows the average scores for each dataset over each combination of word embedding type and distant phase.

Embedding Type	DAI	MPQ	DIL	TAC	SEM	JCR	SEval	HUL	Union	Avg.
Random	0.660	0.499	0.542	0.635	0.460	0.354	0.639	0.563	0.583	0.548
News	0.667	***0.570***	0.540	***0.668***	***0.528***	***0.417***	***0.683***	0.561	0.561	0.577
Twitter	***0.688***	0.521	***0.551***	0.643	0.522	0.385	0.666	***0.573***	***0.602***	0.572
Wikipedia	0.626	0.538	0.515	0.625	0.504	0.414	0.626	0.549	0.575	0.552

(b) Shows the average scores achieved for each word embedding type on each dataset. The last column shows the average score of the word embedding types.

Distant Phase Type	DAI	MPQ	DIL	TAC	SEM	JCR	SEval	HUL	Union	Avg.
None	0.603	0.520	0.489	0.594	0.502	0.351	0.628	0.489	0.579	0.528
Reviews	0.688	***0.546***	***0.589***	***0.694***	0.492	***0.418***	0.662	***0.658***	***0.604***	0.595
Twitter	***0.690***	0.530	0.533	0.640	***0.517***	0.409	***0.669***	0.539	0.558	0.565

(c) Shows the average scores achieved by each distant-phase on each data-set. The last column shows the average score achieved by the distant phase.

Table 5: *Gives an overview of the averaged scores. In Panel A the average score for each dataset is shown. Panel B shows the average scores achieve by each embedding type. Panel C shows the average scores for the distant supervised phases.*

Train \ Test	DAI *T*	MPQ *N*	DIL *R*	TAC *R*	SEM *H*	JCR *Q*	SEval *T*	HUL *R*	Union
DAI T	**0.734**	0.161	0.401	0.369	0.283	0.269	0.554	0.397	0.447
MPQ N	0.495	**0.581**	0.307	0.402	0.313	0.411	0.471	0.318	0.489
DIL R	0.381	0.210	**0.603**	0.478	0.135	0.227	0.365	0.602	0.350
TAC R	0.395	0.376	0.501	**0.714**	0.360	0.409	0.480	0.517	0.442
SEM H	0.360	0.148	0.188	0.247	**0.554**	0.054	0.250	0.181	0.227
JCR Q	0.450	0.319	0.402	0.461	0.254	**0.457**	0.402	0.452	0.384
SEval T	0.525	0.441	0.489	0.577	0.445	0.421	**0.691**	0.479	0.578
HUL R	0.404	0.252	0.567	0.535	0.176	0.312	0.392	**0.666**	0.373
Union	**0.725**	0.55	0.554	0.614	0.422	0.465	0.69	0.528	0.624
FD Avg.	0.43	0.272	0.408	0.438	0.281	0.301	0.416	0.421	0.411
Diff.	0.304	0.308	0.195	0.276	0.273	0.156	0.275	0.245	0.213

Table 8: *Results obtained by training on a target domain (TD) and evaluation on all domains. The line* FD Avg. *shows the average scores for each TD when trained on a foreign domain (FD). The line* Diff. *shows the difference between the best score of TD and FD Avg.*

A general system does not increase the systems prediction power. The results achieved by training on the union of all data and optimizing for a specific TD shows no increase in score on the TD. Only on the *JCR*-quotations the score increased, on the twitter datasets (*DAI* and *SEval*) the score is similar to the score of the target specific system. In all the other cases the systems trained on the union of all data perform worse. In the case of the *HUL*-reviews the drop is even by 14 points.

3.3 Ablation Experiments

To further assess the generalization performance we ran ablation experiments as follows: We combine all the training sets except for the target domain set, train the system on this combination of data, and then evaluate the system on the target domain.

The generalized FD system performs better than a specialized FD system. Table 9 shows the performance of the system trained on the combination of FD data excluding the TD. The results show that in most cases training on a mixture of FD data achieves better scores on the TD data than training using a single FD for training (see Table 8). As expected the general FD system is usually not able to achieve the score on the TD data achieved by the specialized TD system. Table 9 shows the difference between the specialized TD system and the generalized FD system. The differences range from 3 points in the case the *DIL*-reviews up to 17 points for the *MPQ*-news. Only for the *JCR*-quotations the generalized FD system performs better. Thus, it is best to have TD data, although in some cases an acceptable score might be achieved using a generalized FD system.

	Ablation Sys. without TD	Specific TD System	Diff.
DAI	0.658	0.734	0.076
MPQ	0.404	0.581	0.177
DIL	0.573	0.603	0.030
TAC	0.558	0.714	0.156
SEM	0.426	0.554	0.128
JCR	0.485	0.457	-0.029
SEval	0.658	0.691	0.033
HUL	0.566	0.666	0.099

Table 9: *Results of the ablation experiments. The last column shows the difference between the specific TD system and the Ablation System trained on a mix of FD data excluding data from the TD.*

3.4 Augmentation Experiments

To further investigate the difference between a specialized system and a general system we performed experiments where we start with a specialized TD, specialized FD, or a general FD system (referred to as *base system*) and gradually transform it to a generalized system by adding data. Let n be the number of texts used to train the base system. Then we augment the training set by adding $n/2$, n and $2n$ datapoints. The evaluation is always performed on the TD.

Adding FD to a specialized TD system decreases the performance on the target domain. For each of the 8 TDs we start with a specialized TD system and gradually add a combination of FD data (*mixed FD augmentation*) or data from a single FD (*single FD augmentation*) and evaluate the performance on TD. Figure 2 shows the scores averaged over all experiments for each TD. The trend shows that adding more data from one or more FDs for training decreases the performance of the system.

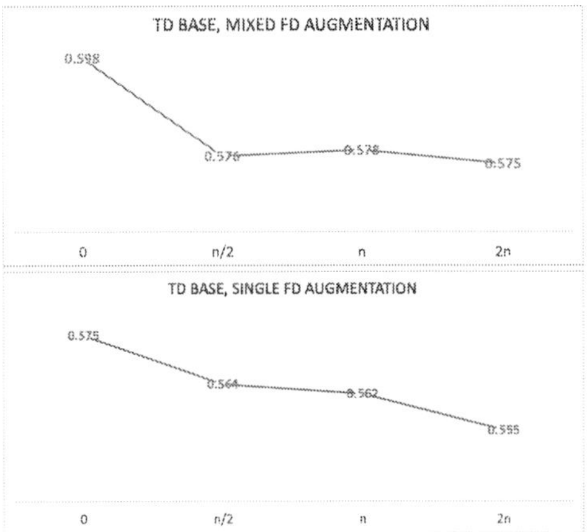

Figure 2: *Averaged F1 scores for the increasing amount of FD (mixed set or single domain set) for a TD data basis.*

Adding TD to a FD system increases the score. For each TD we start with a specialized FD system (*single FD base*) or a generalized FD system (*mix FD base*) and gradually add more data from the TD. In both cases adding more data from the TD increases the performance of the system when it is evaluated on the TD (see Figure 3).

4 Conclusion

In this work we gave an overview of the deterioration of the quality when using a sentiment classifier on a domain it was not trained on. Our in-depth analysis showed that having a large corpus of weakly labelled data boosts the score by 7 points on average. We also showed that using pre-trained word embeddings helps to increase the score by 3-4 points on average. This work can be used as a basis when evaluating sentiment classifiers that were trained on a domain different from the target domain. Future work in this area would include more indepth analysis of the inter-

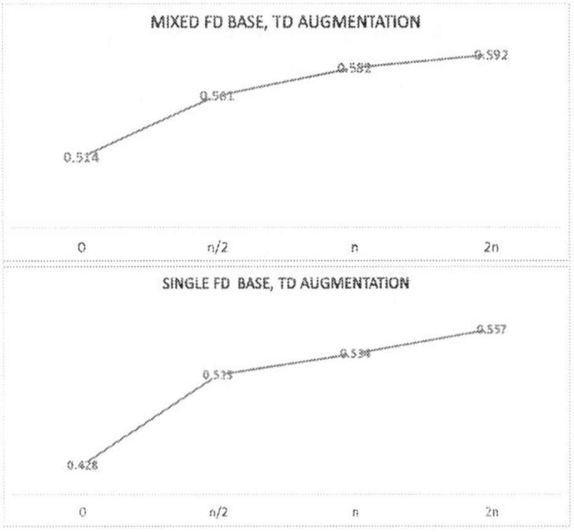

Figure 3: *Averaged F1 for increasing the amount of TD data starting with either a base of mixed FD data or single FD data.*

play among different domains: for instance our results show that a system trained on tweets performs better on reviews than a system trained on news. Here, a better understanding of these mechanisms is necessary to better assess the potential of cross domain classification. Furthermore, one can analyse the effect of the distant-phases and word embeddings in the cross-domain setting. How does the usage of different types of word embeddings and weakly labelled data impact the performance in a cross-domain setting? Does the usage of weakly-labelled data increase the performance of a sentiment classifier on a foreign domain? We are convinced that answering these questions will help to develop sentiment analysis systems that perform better on new, unknown domains.

References

Alexandra Balahur, Ralf Steinberger, Mijail Kabadjov, Vanni Zavarella, Erik Van Der Goot, Matina Halkia, Bruno Pouliquen, and Jenya Belyaeva. 2013. Sentiment analysis in the news. In *Proceedings of the 7th International Conference on Language Resources and Evaluation*, pages 2216–2220. European Language Resources Association.

John Blitzer, Mark Dredze, and Fernanod Pereira. 2007. Biographies, bollywood, boom-boxes and blenders: Domain adaptation for sentiment classification. In *Proceedings of the 45th Annual Meeting of the Association of Computational Linguistics*, pages 187–205. Association for Computational Linguistics.

Danushka Bollegala, David Weir, and John Carroll.

2011. Using multiple sources to construct a sentiment sensitive thesaurus for cross-domain sentiment classification. In *Proceedings of the 49th Annual Meeting of the Association for Computational Linguistics: Human Language Technologies*, pages 132–141. Association for Computational Linguistics.

Danushka Bollegala, Tingting Mu, and John Yanis Goulermas. 2016. Cross-domain sentiment classification using sentiment sensitive embeddings. *IEEE Transactions on Knowledge and Data Engineering*, 28(2):398–410.

Jan Deriu, Maurice Gonzenbach, Fatih Uzdilli, Aurelien Lucchi, Valeria De Luca, and Martin Jaggi. 2016. Swisscheese at semeval-2016 task 4: Sentiment classification using an ensemble of convolutional neural networks with distant supervision. In *Proceedings of the 10th International Workshop on Semantic Evaluation (SemEval-2016)*, pages 1124–1128. Association for Computational Linguistics.

Xiaowen Ding, Bing Liu, and Philip S Yu. 2008. A holistic lexicon-based approach to opinion mining. In *Proceedings of the 2008 international conference on web search and data mining*, pages 231–240. Association for Computing Machinery.

Xavier Glorot, Antoine Bordes, and Yoshua Bengio. 2011. Domain adaptation for large-scale sentiment classification: A deep learning approach. In *Proceedings of the 28th international conference on machine learning (ICML-11)*, pages 513–520.

Minqing Hu and Bing Liu. 2004. Mining and summarizing customer reviews. In *Proceedings of the tenth ACM SIGKDD international conference on Knowledge discovery and data mining*, pages 168–177. Association for Computing Machinery.

Shoushan Li and Chengqing Zong. 2008. Multi-domain sentiment classification. In *Proceedings of the 46th Annual Meeting of the Association for Computational Linguistics on Human Language Technologies: Short Papers*, pages 257–260. Association for Computational Linguistics.

Julian McAuley, Rahul Pandey, and Jure Leskovec. 2015. Inferring networks of substitutable and complementary products. In *Proceedings of the 21th ACM SIGKDD International Conference on Knowledge Discovery and Data Mining*, pages 785–794. Association for Computational Linguistics.

Tomas Mikolov, Ilya Sutskever, Kai Chen, Greg S Corrado, and Jeff Dean. 2013. Distributed representations of words and phrases and their compositionality. In *Advances in neural information processing systems*, pages 3111–3119. Curran Associates, Inc.

Preslav Nakov, Alan Ritter, Sara Rosenthal, Veselin Stoyanov, and Fabrizio Sebastiani. 2016. SemEval-2016 task 4: Sentiment analysis in Twitter. In *Proceedings of the 10th international workshop on semantic evaluation (SemEval 2016)*, pages 1–18. Association for Computational Linguistics.

Sascha Narr, Michael Hulfenhaus, and Sahin Albayrak. 2012. Language-independent twitter sentiment analysis. *Knowledge Discovery and Machine Learning (KDML), LWA*, pages 12–14.

Sinno Jialin Pan, Xiaochuan Ni, Jian-Tao Sun, Qiang Yang, and Zheng Chen. 2010. Cross-domain sentiment classification via spectral feature alignment. In *Proceedings of the 19th international conference on World wide web*, pages 751–760. Association for Computing Machinery.

Aliaksei Severyn and Alessandro Moschitti. 2015. Twitter Sentiment Analysis with Deep Convolutional Neural Networks. In *Proceedings of the 38th International ACM SIGIR Conference on Research and Development in Information Retrieval*, pages 959–962. Association for Computing Machinery.

Carlo Strapparava and Rada Mihalcea. 2007. Semeval-2007 task 14: Affective text. In *Proceedings of the 4th International Workshop on Semantic Evaluations*, pages 70–74. Association for Computational Linguistics.

Oscar Täckström and Ryan McDonald. 2011. Discovering fine-grained sentiment with latent variable structured prediction models. In *In Proceedings of the 33rd European Conference on Advances in Information Retrieval*, pages 368–374. Springer.

Janyce Wiebe, Theresa Wilson, and Claire Cardie. 2005. Annotating expressions of opinions and emotions in language. *Language resources and evaluation*, 39(2-3):165–210.

Jianfei Yu and Jing Jiang. 2016. Learning sentence embeddings with auxiliary tasks for cross-domain sentiment classification. In *Proceedings of the 2016 Conference on Empirical Methods in Natural Language Processing*, pages 236–246, Austin, Texas, November. Association for Computational Linguistics.

Aligning Entity Names with Online Aliases on Twitter

Kevin McKelvey **Peter Goutzounis**
Stephen da Cruz **Nathanael Chambers**
Department of Computer Science
United States Naval Academy
nchamber@usna.edu

Abstract

This paper presents new models that automatically align online aliases with their real entity names. Many research applications rely on identifying entity names in text, but people often refer to entities with unexpected nicknames and aliases. For example, *The King* and *King James* are aliases for *Lebron James*, a professional basketball player. Recent work on entity linking attempts to resolve mentions to knowledge base entries, like a wikipedia page, but linking is unfortunately limited to well-known entities with pre-built pages. This paper asks a more basic question: can aliases be aligned without background knowledge of the entity? Further, can the semantics surrounding alias mentions be used to inform alignments? We describe statistical models that make decisions based on the lexicographic properties of the aliases with their semantic context in a large corpus of tweets. We experiment on a database of Twitter users and their usernames, and present the first human evaluation for this task. Alignment accuracy approaches human performance at 81%, and we show that while lexicographic features are most important, the semantic context of an alias further improves classification accuracy.

1 Introduction

A wide range of research in natural language processing focuses on entities. These range from basic language tasks like coreference resolution to broader aggregation applications like sentiment analysis and information extraction. Building an accurate picture of an entity (e.g., aggregate sentiment toward the entity, entity tracking across websites, database population) requires an understanding of all the varying ways people refer to that entity. Tracking "facebook" is not enough to know how people feel about it, as mentions of "fbook", "FB", and "the book" also need to be understood. Although many applications exist for tracking known mentions of entities, less research exists for detecting nicknames and aliases.

This paper presents new models to align an entity's name (e.g., "Bank of America") with its online aliases ("BAmerica") and nicknames ("BofA"). Unlike the traditional *entity linking* task that relies on known knowledge base (KB) entries, our task is unique by removing the assumption that a KB is available for each entity. Instead, we simply begin with an entity name and an alias, and ask if the two are likely to refer to the same real-world entity. By asking this more basic question first, several research threads will benefit.

For instance, aligning entity names is important to *sentiment analysis*, but typically ignored for simplification reasons. Companies track social media for mentions of their company in hopes of identifying the public sentiment toward them. Political races rely on similar models, tracking mentions of politicians ("Trump" might be negatively referred to as "Frump"). Research on contextual sentiment analysis has exploded as a result, but the vast majority assumes a single known entity name. In fact, this paper's work originally came about because the authors wanted to track events surrounding 'Bank of America', but we kept coming across unexpected new aliases that referred to the company.

Another application is *user profiling* across websites. User accounts that span multiple websites often use different usernames. Most research in this area has focused on aligning account attributes and graph structure. This paper con-

Proceedings of the Fifth International Workshop on Natural Language Processing for Social Media , pages 25–35,
Valencia, Spain, April 3-7, 2017. ©2017 Association for Computational Linguistics

tributes by first addressing the more basic challenge of username alignment.

Finally, this paper also furthers research in *event detection*. If a subset of users on Twitter are talking about a *Katy Perry* concert next week, the task is to extract the date and artist. However, are they referring to the same concert when other users mention *Fruit Sister*? Still others might discuss *Katey Parry* (a misspelling) and *Katherine Hudson* (previous name)? Despite the popularity of this artist, some of these names don't exist in preconstructed KBs. The challenge is exacerbated when the target artist is relatively unknown. This paper experiments with new learning models to align examples like these using only the corpus in which they appear.

The first set of models rely on purely lexicographic characteristics. We propose a series of character and word-based features, trained with discriminative classifiers. Many aliases share obvious characteristics, such as acronym usage and word shortening. These models learn the patterns used when people create nicknames.

The second set of models take a distributional semantics approach. Names like *fruit sister* and *katy perry* have no obvious lexical overlap, so the task of aligning the aliases is impossible without understanding their usage in language. We first present experiments with distributional word vectors to represent the context of aliases, and then measure vector similarity to inform the alignment decision. We then round off the contextual approach with word embeddings from recent neural network research in NLP.

To our knowledge, these are the first machine learned models that align entity names without prior knowledge of the entities. Further, we describe the first human study to measure task difficulty and compare model performance. The lexical and semantic models approach human performance on the task.

2 Previous Work

This paper aligns entity names ("Shem Ayegba") to their aliases ("shemo4real"). Relevant previous work falls into three categories: detecting attributes of online users, entity linking, and user linking.

A large body of work has looked into **attribute detection** of social media users, particularly those on Twitter. Given a particular user, what is that person's age (Nguyen et al., 2013), gender, education background, political orientation, ethnicity (Bergsma et al., 2013), etc. This paper is related in learning a different type of attribute: aliases and nicknames.

Early experiments on attribute detection rely on a user's text (e.g., tweets) to predict a range of different attributes (Rao et al., 2010). Many build learning models that are applicable across a variety of different user attributes (Chen et al., 2015a; Volkova et al., 2015; Beretta et al., 2015). Among the attributes, political preferences is a frequent area of research, again relying on features from user tweets, and making use of graph-based algorithms over their friends' attributes (Golbeck and Hansen, 2011; Conover et al., 2011; Wong et al., 2013; Cohen and Ruths, 2013; Volkova et al., 2014). Pla et al. (2014) even uses sentiment analysis.

This paper is related to attribute extraction in the desire to learn about an online user. However, the task at hand is to resolve *mentions* of a user's online alias (i.e., twitter handle) and *mentions* of a named entity (i.e., a business or a person's real name). Unlike the body of work on attribute extraction, we assume we do not have an entity's body of published text, but instead just observed their name in text.

More related to our goal of name understanding is research on gender identification (Rao et al., 2010; Burger et al., 2011; Van Durme, 2012; Filippova, 2012; Ciot et al., 2013). In many of these, the name of a user is informative. Most work thus uses the name as an indicator, but then also uses the user's text posts to assist. The name itself offers insight into this answer, and some models rely first on dictionaries of names before backing off to a machine learner trained on user tweets (Liu and Ruths, 2013; Volkova and Yarowsky, 2014).

Chen et al. (Chen et al., 2015b) pursued a novel line of investigation which uses only a user's name, and infers *visual attributes* by using click-through data on name searches and web images. Although very different in the type of predicted knowledge, this paper is similar in that we only have a name and must infer properties of that person, namely *who* it is in real life.

Others have studied whether gender and language can be identified from only the username. They looked at characters and morphological units with an unsupervised learning approach (Jaech and Ostendorf, 2015). This paper is similar in challenge in that we also start with only the user's name, but the methods are very different.

This paper is also a new form of **entity linking**. Entity linking is an active research field that aims to resolve an entity mention (e.g., "michael jordan") to an entry in a knowledge base (e.g., michael jordan's wikipedia page). Most work in this field relies on the text context around the mention to measure similarity with the text description of the entity in the KB, such as a wikipedia entry's text (Adafre and de Rijke, 2005; Bunescu and Pasca, 2006; Mihalcea and Csomai, 2007; Milne and Witten, 2008; Dredze et al., 2010; Ratinov et al., 2011; Han et al., 2011; Demartini et al., 2012; Moro et al., 2014; Moro and Navigli, 2015). All of these papers assume they have knowledge base entries with text to assist in resolving entity mentions. This paper is different in that we don't have a knowledge base, but just an online alias. We start from the assumption that we don't have text from that alias, and must rely solely on observed mentions and properties of the name/alias itself.

Finally, **user linking** across website communities is an active research area. Research typically focuses on finding similarities in the social network structure (Backstrom et al., 2007; Narayanan and Shmatikov, 2009; Tan et al., 2014; Liu et al., 2016), similar user attributes across the sites (Li and Lin, 2014; Goga, 2014; Zafarani et al., 2015; Goga et al., 2015; Naini et al., 2016), or both (Liu et al., 2014; Chung et al., 2014). Not many focus on usernames, with the exception of Liu et al. (2013), but they study how to identify different users who use *the same username*. Very recently, Wang et al. (2016) describe a heuristic text comparison model between different usernames. While similar in goal to this paper, we apply a far wider range of features, incorporate semantic knowledge, and use modern machine learning techniques.

3 Datasets

The main experiment dataset is a list of name/alias pairs. Table 1 shows a few examples of these pairs. The list is comprised of approximately 110k pairs of names and their actual twitter handles extracted from a single day of tweets in November 2015. We selected 110k tweets, and paired the name listed on the profile of the user who wrote the tweet with the same user's twitter handle. This name/handle pair is a single datum in the dataset.

Profile Name	**Twitter Handle**
Shem Ayegba	@shemo4real
mimi sanson viola	@palomahepzibah
Alisha	@alishajii
The Hammer of Facts	@FactsHammer
John Kielbowicz	@kibblebits

Table 1: Examples of name/handle pairs in the dataset.

We then generated another 110k *false* pairs by randomly selecting twitter handles and matching them with incorrect profile names. Combined with the correct 110k pairs, the resulting dataset is 220k name/alias pairs, half of which are correct and half incorrect. This list is then broken up into 160k pairs for training, 40k for a held-out test set, and 20k for a development set. Finally, we remove all pairs in the test set that contain a username or a handle that also appears in the training set. This avoids all overlap between train and test. A very minor reduction in test set size resulted from this.

Since our experiments rely on corpus-based features, we use one year of tweets from the freely available Twitter streaming API from Aug 2014 to Aug 2015. We refer to this corpus later as our "one-year tweet corpus".

4 Models

We model the discovery of online aliases for a real name as a pairwise classification task. Given an entity's name and a single alias, what is the probability that the two refer to the same entity? This pairwise classifier can then be employed in a variety of practical systems, such as producing a ranked list of likely names for an alias, or the inverse problem of identifying the most likely alias for a target entity.

4.1 Learning Models

We experimented with both support vector machines (SVM) and maximum entropy classifiers. The input is an entity name and alias pair $x = (e, a)$ that is mapped to a set of features $f(x)$, described next. We used the Stanford CoreNLP toolkit [1] for implementations of the models using the software's default parameters.

[1]http://stanfordnlp.github.io/CoreNLP/

4.2 Lexicographic Features

The primary features for a name/alias pair are based on the characters and string commonalities between the two. We experimented with thirteen such lexicographic features.

Edit Distance. This feature uses the Levenshtein edit distance between the name and alias. This computes the number of character additions, deletions, and substitutions that are required to turn the alias into the name. The name and alias are both lowercased first, and the @ symbol removed from the alias. White space is included in the comparison. The feature returns $1.0 - editdist(n, a)$. The higher the value, the more similar the strings.

Exact Match. If the lowercased name and alias are exact matches after white space is removed, this binary feature is turned on.

First and Last Name. Three features were developed based on an entity having a first and last name. If the alias starts with the first name of the entity, the feature returns the length of that name. The last name feature is the same, but looking instead for the last name. A third feature is a binary feature that indicates if the entity name appears in whole (with spaces removed) anywhere in the alias. For example, *John Williams* occurs in the twitter handle, *@JohnWilliams2*.

Percent Substring. Returns the number of overlapping characters between the alias and name, divided by the length of the name. This is a representation of the percentage of an alias that contains a name. However, this feature is not case-sensitive nor sequential, meaning that the position of the characters does not matter, only their presence is accounted for.

Starts and Ends With. These are two distinct features. Starts-with compares the lowercased alias-name pair and returns the count of overlapping characters in the longest shared prefix. The ends-with feature is the same, but instead counts the longest shared suffix.

Capital Substring. This feature splits the alias into substrings based on capital letters, and returns the number of such substrings that are contained within the name (not necessarily capitalized).

Acronyms. Two features: if the alias is an acronym of the lowercased name's tokens, the binary acronym feature is turned on. Second, a capital-acronym feature compares the number of capital letters in the name that occur in the alias. This feature is the number of overlapping matches.

Exact Capitalization. Capitalization is a binary feature that compares the capital letters of a name to the capital letters of an alias and returns true on an identical match. This overlaps in purpose with the acronym features, but it captures a broader set.

Reverse Substring. This is a binary feature that returns true if the alias is the name in reverse, or vice-versa. This was inspired by examples like *Janey* and *@yenaj*.

Unused Lexicographic Features. Two lexical features were ultimately abandoned: one-word-substring and semi-acronym. One-word-substring returns the length of any one word in the entity that was contained in the handle. Semi-acronym attempted to construct acronyms using full prepositions (i.e. "BofA"). Neither had a positive effect on development set results.

4.3 Semantic Features

The above lexical features approximate what is available to a naïve user/system who is presented with a name/alias pair. Overlap and similarity of the characters is the only available means to make a decision, and if the name and alias share little similarity, there is no remaining recourse to fall back on.

This section describes our attempts at broadening the learning model into shallow semantics by making use of a large corpus of tweets. Semantic similarity has a rich history in computational semantics of representing words with *context vectors*. This is often called distributional semantics where a word (or a name in our case) *is known by the company it keeps* (Firth, 1957). We follow the traditional approach by representing a name (or alias) by a vector of word counts from the words seen in tweets surrounding the name. The following shows a tweet with entity *Dominic Dyer*, and the corresponding context vector.

> **Tweet**
> The launch of the new book by **Dominic Dyer** at Birdfair today.
>
> **Context Vector**
> (the 2, launch 1, of 1, new 1, book 1, by 1, at 1, Birdfair 1, today 1)

We use the one-year tweet corpus to compute context vectors for each name and alias. All observed mentions of a name (or alias) are summed into its single aggregate semantic context vector.

Word Vectors. Each entity and alias has a context word vector, as described above. All context tokens were lowercased, and leading/trailing punctuation removed. We then created three features using the vectors: binary, cosine, and averaged-cosine variants. The **cosine** feature is the traditional context vector feature: compute the cosine between the name's vector and the alias' vector. The **binary** feature is a binarized version of cosine, true if the cosine is greater than 0.1 and false otherwise. The **averaged-cosine** feature is motivated by the observation that large vectors tend to result in higher cosine scores (more likely to contain overlapping tokens). This feature returns the difference between an entity's average cosine score and its cosine score with the alias in question:

$$f(n, a) = \frac{cos(n, a) * N}{\sum_x cos(n, x)} - 1 \quad (1)$$

where n is the name vector, a is the alias vector, and N is the number of aliases. If the $cos(n, a)$ is bigger than average, this equation returns a value greater than 0.

Word Embeddings. Recent work on neural networks have shown *word embeddings* to outperform traditional context vectors on a variety of NLP tasks. We thus trained a skip-gram neural net on our twitter data, and created word embeddings for the entity names and aliases. The open-source Word2Vec from deeplearning4j was used as the model implementation[2]. Word2Vec implements a skip-gram neural model where the input is the target word (or entity name), and predicted output are the words to the left and right of the target. A word's embedding is the vector of weights for the hidden layer. The implementation is based on Mikolov et al. (2013).

Once word embeddings are learned for all observed names and aliases, we duplicate the three word vector features described above. Since word embeddings are also vectors, the features are implemented the same.

[2]http://deeplearning4j.org/word2vec

5 Experiments

We focus on the basic task of predicting whether an alias belongs to a name, given only a corpus of tweets and no other entity knowledge. Experiments use the name/alias pairs as described above in Datasets. Given a name/alias pair, the task is to predict "yes" or "no" to whether the two mentions likely refer to the same entity. As a binary prediction task, the random baseline is 50% accuracy. Each name in the dataset appears in both one correct pair with its true twitter handle, and one incorrect pair with a randomly selected twitter handle.

We use accuracy as the evaluation metric with its normal definition:

$$Accuracy = \frac{\#correct}{N} \quad (2)$$

where N is the size of the evaluation set.

We report accuracy on the entire evaluation set (**Accuracy: all**) as well as a subset of the evaluation that includes only entity pairs such that the entity name and the twitter handle were each seen at least 100 times in the one-year twitter corpus (**Accuracy: 100**). This second set serves the purpose of distinguishing the importance of frequency when using semantic vector features. Entity mentions that rarely occur have sparse vectors, and a prediction relies solely on the lexicographic features.

The features in the models were developed on the training and development sets only. We report on several feature ablation tests on the development set. Feature ablation was not conducted on the test set. The test set was only used to generate the final results table.

Both SVM and MaxEnt models used the default settings in CoreNLP, but we only report MaxEnt results as neither significantly outperformed the other.

Four baseline models are included to illustrate the non-trivial nature of this task. At first blush, it may appear that this paper's focus is a trivial string match. Part of the motivation for this paper's focus is to illustrate how even the most basic of username mapping tasks is non-trivial. The first baseline, **Simple-Match**, simply lowercases and removes white space from both the name and alias. If the two changed strings now match exactly, then the baseline predicts match. The second baseline, **Alpha-Match**, is a variation of Simple-Match, but also removes all characters not in the a-z alphabet (e.g., 'david' and '88david-2' match). The third baseline, **Alpha-RelaxMatch** relaxes Alpha-Match by only requiring the first 5 characters in both name and alias to match. Finally, the fourth baseline is a machine learned model using only the edit distance feature (**Edit-Dist**) on lowercased and white-space condensed strings.

Finally, we ran a human evaluation to measure ideal performance on this task. We randomly selected 2,010 pairs from the bigger test set, and several undergraduates were asked to judge whether each name/alias pair was likely or not to be the same entity. We ran our best models on this same smaller test set and report accuracy.

6 Results

Table 2 shows results on the development set for the basic model with additional character-based features. The **Simple-Match** baseline performs surprisingly low at 57.66%, **Alpha-Match** slightly better, and **Alpha-RelaxMatch** the best baseline at 69.57%. Entity names and their twitter handles are not often clear matches. The machine learned baseline that uses only edit distance somewhat surprising barely performs better than random chance.

The most important feature is **first** and **last name** matching, increasing accuracy from 57.66% to 72.44%. These features match if the entity's first (last) name appears at the start (end) of the alias. Other features with further 4% gains each are the percent substring feature, and the numeric feature "starts with" (or "ends with") that returns prefix or suffix matches. This partly overlaps with the first name feature, but is more general and significantly improves performance.

The above experiment only had access to an entity's name and possible alias. The best classifier with just lexicographic features is 81.63% accurate. The next experiment expands to assume the availability of a corpus with entity mentions. Starting with distributional word vectors, Table 3 shows the performance on the subset of data where the entity mention was seen at least 100 times. Word vectors are useless for new and rare mentions, so we focus on the portion of data where vectors are applicable. The word vector features combine for a 1.4% relative gain.

Though a small gain, for insight into how these features might help, see Figure 1 for the top token

Development Set Accuracy

	Acc: All	Acc: 100
Base (Simple-Match)	57.66	45.24
Base (Alpha-Match)	61.72	47.62
Base (Alpha-RMatch)	69.57	54.76
Base (ML Edit-Dist)	57.66	45.24
+first-last	72.44	59.62
+percent substring	77.02	62.00
+starts-ends	81.06	67.46
+acronyms	81.16	67.6
+all lexical feats	81.63	70.93

Table 2: Development set results and feature comparison. Numbers are % accuracy: 81.6 and 70.9

Dev Set Accuracy with Word Vectors

	Accuracy: 100
All Lexical	70.93%
w/ binary word vector	71.92%
w/ cosine word vector	72.22%
w/ average word vector	70.93%
+ all vector features	**71.93%**

Table 3: Word vector accuracy on the development set. Each row is the feature by itself without the other vector features. The final row is the inclusion of all three features in one learned model.

Test Set Accuracy

	Acc: All	Acc: 100
Base (Simple-Match)	54.63	42.02
Base (Edit-Dist)	56.80	50.08
Base (Alpha-Match)	58.98	44.94
Base (Alpha-RMatch)	67.33	52.25
All Lexical	80.73	71.60
+binary word vec	80.82	72.59
+cosine word vec	80.81	72.47
+average word vec	80.73	71.60
+all vec features	**80.83**	**72.59**

Table 4: Word vector accuracy results on the Test set. All features are included.

Test Set Accuracy with Embeddings

	Acc: All	Acc: 100
All Lexical	80.73	71.60
Lexical+vector	80.83	72.59
Lexical+embed	80.71	71.2T0

Table 5: Accuracy on the Test set when adding word embedding features.

counts in entity/alias vectors. Word context can capture their typical contexts as long as they occur in the corpus.

After developing features on the dev set, we ran the same feature ablation one time on the test set. Results are shown in Table 4. The improvement from the individual word vector features is similar to the development set, confirming that we did not overfit model development. The final relative improvement on the Accuracy:100 set is again 1.4% over the lexical-only model. This improvement is statistically significant ($p < 0.000001$, McNemar's test, 2-tailed).

We also tested word embeddings as a substitute feature for distributional word vectors. We trained our own embeddings for each entity string and twitter handle using word2vec. Table 5 shows the results as virtually identical to the distributional vectors. The two essentially capture the same information in this particular task as including both types of features offered no further gain.

Table 6 gives precision and recall for correctly guessing *yes* and *no* as individual labels.

Finally, Table 7 shows human performance compared to our best model. The two are virtually the same at 81% accuracy. The all lexical model is able to capture the same knowledge a typical human brings to identifying likely aliases of new entities.

Precision and Recall Comparison

	Match		Non	
	P	**R**	**P**	**R**
Simple-Match	100	13.1	51.3	100
All Lexical	93.5	67.8	72.9	94.8
All Lexical + vec	92.8	68.5	73.2	94.2

Table 6: Precision and Recall on the Test set for correctly identifying alignment pairs.

Human Evaluation Test Set

	Accuracy
Baseline (Edit-Dist)	49.03
Baseline (Simple-Match)	56.14
All Lexical + vector	80.96
Human	**81.01**

Table 7: Human evaluation comparison on a separate test set of approximately 2000 pairs.

7 Error Analysis

Several questions hide behind the accuracy numbers. We briefly address a few of them here.

7.1 Why is accuracy for high frequency entities lower?

The results for **Acc:100** in the result tables are significantly lower than the **Acc:All** results. These are the entities that occurred at least 100 times in our one year corpus, so they represent entities that are discussed more frequently than others. The best baseline at 67% on Test drops to only 52% for this subset of frequent entities.

The main reason for high frequency entities to be more difficult appears to be due to the fact that high frequency entities have less similarity in their twitter handles. We computed the edit distance between each entity's name and handle, dividing by the length of the entity string. The average normalized edit distance across all development set pairs is **0.97**. Computing this normalized edit distance for only entities occurring 100 or more times, and the average is twice as high at **1.84**. The direct answer for why high frequency entities are more difficult is that their profile names have far less in common with their twitter handles. But why?

Manual error analysis revealed that high frequency entities often have short profile names.

dominic dyer	**URL**, **born**, **badger**, anneka, svenska, lionaid, #lionsbetrayed, #bantrophyhunting, interviewed, tells, **trust**, bbc, ceo, speech, @badgertrust, ...
@domdyer70	**URL**, **badger**, london, join, march, cull, protest, wildlife, **trust**, badgers, against, army, saturday, @lionaid, **born**, ...
@CraftsmenLtd	**URL**, @poppyscupcakes, #ff, #creativebizhour, @etsy, cupcakes, mock, clever, @lizzie_chantree, @sweettoothmarti, @chichicardsuk, vine, #handmadehour, ...

Figure 1: Word vectors for an entity and two possible aliases. *@domdyer70* is correct for *dominic dyer*.

This surprised the authors as we assumed uniform behavior in profile names. It turns out that many frequently mentioned online entities have *shorter profile names*, most likely due to their popularity. Our manual analysis shows that many of these use only given names or nicknames, avoiding surnames. When someone is less known, they perhaps prefer a full name to distinguish who they are. Once someone is known, shorter names become a benefit of the popularity. However, this shorter name behavior does *not* transfer to the twitter handle. Since twitter handles must be unique across all users, short names are unavailable and tend to be longer for everyone. This appears to explain most of why so many more edits are required in the edit distance computation of high frequency entities.

High frequency entities are more difficult because they contain less lexicographic overalp due to conciseness of their profile names. This also explains why the trained classifier performs lower based on only character-based features. This leads us to analyze the non-character context vectors.

7.2 Do context vectors actually help?

The 1.4% relative improvement on Test when adding context vectors is not particularly impressive, though the improvement is statistically significant (using McNemar's test) on the test set. One possible explanation for the smaller gain is that word vectors do help, but they help on the same entity/alias pairs that lexical features already correctly classify. To test this reasoning, we trained the model with only word vector features and wihtout the full lexical model. Do context vectors improve over the baselines?

Table 8 shows their accuracy on the Test set is **57.16%**. Note that this vector-only model completely ignores character-level similarity between the entity's name and alias. If the name is "david" and the alias is "@david2", this trained model does not take that into account. The features only compare the contexts observed around those two mentions in the corpus. Its performance is a 14% relative increase over a random baseline, and notably, almost 10% relative over our strongest baseline (Alpha-RelaxedMatch, comparing the name and alias strings).

	Acc: 100
Baseline (Random Guess)	50.00
Baseline (Alpha-RMatch)	52.25
Trained only w/ context vecs	**57.16%**

Table 8: Measuring performance of the word context vector features by themselves as the only classifier input. Accuracy is reported on the pairs seen at least 100 times in the corpus.

Clearly the context vectors do provide a useful signal, albeit less of a contribution when the full lexical information is also included.

7.3 What types of errors remain to be solved?

The main observed error occurs when the alias has no overt lexical relation to its true entity name **and** they rarely occur in the corpus. Some examples are given here (these are correct names with their twitter handles):

Nicola @Luckyminx79
Avery @moodyscience
Tobin Heath @lanaxjauregui
Amanda @bieberfto21
Manuel @angel1110497

Without lexical clues, and no word context vector due to sparsity, our models fail. Humans obviously fail too. Our results around 80% accuracy suggest a ceiling of 20% of the data contains these errors. A far more complex and resource-heavy model that can spider alias feeds, conversations, and profiles to build a user profile is required. Section 2 discusses several relevant works. In regards to this paper's core question (can we resolve aliases without pre-knowledge of entities?), these errors are not addressed.

8 Discussion

This is the first proposal, to our knowledge, to align entity mentions with their online aliases *without prior knowledge of the entities*. While similar in spirit to *entity linking*, there is no knowledge base with a grounded referent. The challenge instead is to resolve the plethora of ways people refer to the same person or organization. It is a stripped down, base task, aimed at experimenting with how accurate such a knowledge-light model can be. We aimed to experiment with the bare minimum knowledge.

We found that prediction actually approaches *human-level* performance when using a rich set of lexicographic features. This is perhaps unsurprising because humans don't have background knowledge of random online users, so they also rely solely on lexical observations. It is encouraging that our models approximate some of this reasoning, although even humans only achieve 81% accuracy on this task.

Semantic word vectors achieved a slight increase in accuracy over the lexical model, but were shown useful when used as features by themselves. This suggests other tasks may benefit from building context representations for their entities. One important caveat is that the increased performance is only for entities seen frequently, otherwise semantic context cannot be extracted.

By simplifying the resolution task to pairwise comparison, we believe this work benefits a number of research areas. This paper is perhaps not a practical task by itself, but a very useful first tool. We will release the code as an easy-to-use API (as well as the data). First, it can be used as a plugin to improve *user linking* across websites, comparing user names and profile names ahead of time. Second, entity linking might benefit as another input on top of the usual suite of features. Many papers ignore mention comparison and only focus on context, but our results suggest that a fresh look at mention names is needed. Third, and perhaps most significant, contextual sentiment analysis can be expanded beyond keyword search. Instead of a strict entity match, a broader net can be cast to include the nicknames and aliases of the desired entity. The authors are already leveraging it for this purpose.

The training and test data used in this paper's experiments can be accessed online at www.usna.edu/Users/cs/nchamber. We hope that its release will assist related research needs.

Acknowledgments

This work was supported by a grant from the Office of Naval Research, and a grant from the DoD HPC Modernization Program Office.

References

Sisay Fissaha Adafre and Maarten de Rijke. 2005. Discovering missing links in wikipedia. In *Proceedings of the 3rd international workshop on Link discovery*, pages 90–97.

Lars Backstrom, Cynthia Dwork, and Jon Kleinberg. 2007. Wherefore art thou r3579x?: anonymized social networks, hidden patterns, and structural steganography. In *Proceedings of the 16th international conference on World Wide Web*, pages 181–190.

Valentina Beretta, Daniele Maccagnola, Timothy Cribbin, and Enza Messina. 2015. An interactive method for inferring demographic attributes in twitter. In *Proceedings of the 26th ACM Conference on Hypertext & Social Media*, pages 113–122.

Shane Bergsma, Mark Dredze, Benjamin Van Durme, Theresa Wilson, and David Yarowsky. 2013. Broadly improving user classification via communication-based name and location clustering on twitter. In *Proceedings of the Conference on Human Languate Technologies (HLT-NAACL)*, pages 1010–1019.

Razvan C. Bunescu and Marius Pasca. 2006. Using encyclopedic knowledge for named entity disambiguation. In *Proceedings of the European Chapter of the Association on Computational Linguistics (EACL)*, volume 6, pages 9–16.

John D. Burger, John Henderson, George Kim, and Guido Zarrella. 2011. Discriminating gender on twitter. In *Proceedings of the Conference on Empirical Methods in Natural Language Processing*, pages 1301–1309. Association for Computational Linguistics.

Xin Chen, Yu Wang, Eugene Agichtein, and Fusheng Wang. 2015a. A comparative study of demographic attribute inference in twitter. *Proceedings of the International Conference on Web and Social Media*, pages 590–593.

Yan-Ying Chen, Yin-Hsi Kuo, Chun-Che Wu, and Winston H. Hsu. 2015b. Visually interpreting names as demographic attributes by exploiting click-through data. In *Proceedings of the Twenty-Ninth AAAI Conference on Artificial Intelligence*, pages 44–50. AAAI Press.

Cheng Ta Chung, Chia Jui Lin, Chih Hung Lin, and Pu Jen Cheng. 2014. Person identification between different online social networks. In *Proceedings of the 2014 IEEE/WIC/ACM International Joint Conferences on Web Intelligence (WI) and Intelligent Agent Technologies (IAT)-Volume 01*, pages 94–101. IEEE Computer Society.

Morgane Ciot, Morgan Sonderegger, and Derek Ruths. 2013. Gender inference of twitter users in non-english contexts. In *Proceedings of the Conference on Empirical Methods in Natural Language Processing*, pages 1136–1145.

Raviv Cohen and Derek Ruths. 2013. Classifying political orientation on twitter: It's not easy! In *Proceedings of the International Conference on Web and Social Media*, pages 91–99.

Michael D. Conover, Bruno Gonçalves, Jacob Ratkiewicz, Alessandro Flammini, and Filippo Menczer. 2011. Predicting the political alignment of twitter users. In *Privacy, Security, Risk and Trust (PASSAT) and 2011 IEEE Third Inernational Conference on Social Computing (SocialCom), 2011 IEEE Third International Conference on*, pages 192–199. IEEE.

Gianluca Demartini, Djellel Eddine Difallah, and Philippe Cudré-Mauroux. 2012. Zencrowd: leveraging probabilistic reasoning and crowdsourcing techniques for large-scale entity linking. In *Proceedings of the 21st international conference on World Wide Web*, pages 469–478.

Mark Dredze, Paul McNamee, Delip Rao, Adam Gerber, and Tim Finin. 2010. Entity disambiguation for knowledge base population. In *Proceedings of the 23rd International Conference on Computational Linguistics*, pages 277–285. Association for Computational Linguistics.

Katja Filippova. 2012. User demographics and language in an implicit social network. In *Proceedings of the 2012 Joint Conference on Empirical Methods in Natural Language Processing and Computational Natural Language Learning (EMNLP-CoNLL)*, page 1478–1488.

J. R. Firth. 1957. A synopsis of linguistic theory, 1930-1955. *Studies in Linguistic Analysis*.

Oana Goga, Patrick Loiseau, Robin Sommer, Renata Teixeira, and Krishna P. Gummadi. 2015. On the reliability of profile matching across large online social networks. In *Proceedings of the 21th ACM SIGKDD International Conference on Knowledge Discovery and Data Mining*, pages 1799–1808.

Oana Goga. 2014. *Matching user accounts across online social networks: methods and applications*. Ph.D. thesis, LIP6-Laboratoire d'Informatique de Paris 6.

Jennifer Golbeck and Derek Hansen. 2011. Computing political preference among twitter followers. In *Proceedings of the SIGCHI Conference on Human Factors in Computing Systems*, pages 1105–1108.

Xianpei Han, Le Sun, and Jun Zhao. 2011. Collective entity linking in web text: a graph-based method. In *Proceedings of the 34th international ACM SIGIR conference on Research and development in Information Retrieval*, pages 765–774.

Aaron Jaech and Mari Ostendorf. 2015. What your username says about you. In *Proceedings of the Conference on Empirical Methods in Natural Language Processing*, pages 2032–2037.

Chung-Yi Li and Shou-De Lin. 2014. Matching users and items across domains to improve the recommendation quality. In *Proceedings of the 20th ACM SIGKDD international conference on Knowledge discovery and data mining*, pages 801–810.

Wendy Liu and Derek Ruths. 2013. What's in a name? using first names as features for gender inference in twitter. In *AAAI spring symposium: Analyzing microtext*, volume 13, pages 10–16.

Jing Liu, Fan Zhang, Xinying Song, Young-In Song, Chin-Yew Lin, and Hsiao-Wuen Hon. 2013. What's in a name?: an unsupervised approach to link users across communities. In *Proceedings of the sixth ACM international conference on Web search and data mining*, pages 495–504.

Siyuan Liu, Shuhui Wang, Feida Zhu, Jinbo Zhang, and Ramayya Krishnan. 2014. Hydra: Large-scale social identity linkage via heterogeneous behavior modeling. In *Proceedings of the 2014 ACM SIGMOD international conference on Management of data*, pages 51–62.

Li Liu, William K. Cheung, Xin Li, and Lejian Liao. 2016. Aligning users across social networks using network embedding. In *Proceedings of the Twenty-Fifth International Joint Conference on Artificial Intelligence (IJCAI-16)*, pages 1774–1780.

Rada Mihalcea and Andras Csomai. 2007. Wikify!: linking documents to encyclopedic knowledge. In *Proceedings of the sixteenth ACM conference on Conference on information and knowledge management*, pages 233–242.

Tomas Mikolov, Ilya Sutskever, Kai Chen, Greg S. Corrado, and Jeff Dean. 2013. Distributed representations of words and phrases and their compositionality. In *Advances in neural information processing systems*, pages 3111–3119.

David Milne and Ian H. Witten. 2008. Learning to link with wikipedia. In *ACM Conference on Information and Knowledge Management*, pages 509–518.

Andrea Moro and Roberto Navigli. 2015. Semeval-2015 task 13: multilingual all-words sense disambiguation and entity linking. *Proceedings of SemEval-2015*, pages 288–297.

Andrea Moro, Alessandro Raganato, and Roberto Navigli. 2014. Entity linking meets word sense disambiguation: a unified approach. *Transactions of the Association for Computational Linguistics*, 2:231–244.

Farid M. Naini, Jayakrishnan Unnikrishnan, Patrick Thiran, and Martin Vetterli. 2016. Where you are is who you are: User identification by matching statistics. *IEEE Transactions on Information Forensics and Security*, 11(2):358–372.

Arvind Narayanan and Vitaly Shmatikov. 2009. De-anonymizing social networks. In *2009 30th IEEE symposium on security and privacy*, pages 173–187. IEEE.

Dong-Phuong Nguyen, Rilana Gravel, R.B. Trieschnigg, and Theo Meder. 2013. "how old do you think i am?" a study of language and age in twitter. In *Proceedings of the Seventh International AAAI Conference on Weblogs and Social Media*. AAAI Press.

Ferran Pla and Lluís F. Hurtado. 2014. Political tendency identification in twitter using sentiment analysis techniques. In *Proceedings of the International Conference on Computational Linguistics*, pages 183–192.

Delip Rao, David Yarowsky, Abhishek Shreevats, and Manaswi Gupta. 2010. Classifying latent user attributes in twitter. In *Proceedings of the 2nd international workshop on Search and mining user-generated contents*, pages 37–44.

Lev Ratinov, Dan Roth, Doug Downey, and Mike Anderson. 2011. Local and global algorithms for disambiguation to wikipedia. In *Association for Computational Linguistics: Human Language Technologies*, pages 1375–1384.

Shulong Tan, Ziyu Guan, Deng Cai, Xuzhen Qin, Jiajun Bu, and Chun Chen. 2014. Mapping users across networks by manifold alignment on hypergraph. In *AAAI*, volume 14, pages 159–165. AAAI Press.

Benjamin Van Durme. 2012. Streaming analysis of discourse participants. In *Proceedings of the 2012 Joint Conference on Empirical Methods in Natural Language Processing and Computational Natural Language Learning*, pages 48–58. Association for Computational Linguistics.

Svitlana Volkova and David Yarowsky. 2014. Improving gender prediction of social media users via weighted annotator rationales. In *NIPS 2014 Workshop on Personalization*.

Svitlana Volkova, Glen Coppersmith, and Benjamin Van Durme. 2014. Inferring user political preferences from streaming communications. In *Proceedings of the Association for Computational Linguistics*, pages 186–196.

Svitlana Volkova, Yoram Bachrach, Michael Armstrong, and Vijay Sharma. 2015. Inferring latent user properties from texts published in social media. In *AAAI*, pages 4296–4297. AAAI Press.

Yubin Wang, Tingwen Liu, Qingfeng Tan, Jinqiao Shi, and Li Guo. 2016. Identifying users across different sites using usernames. *Procedia Computer Science*, 80:376–385.

Felix Ming Fai Wong, Chee Wei Tan, Soumya Sen, and Mung Chiang. 2013. Quantifying political leaning from tweets and retweets. *Proceedings of the International Conference on Web and Social Media*, 13:640–649.

Reza Zafarani, Lei Tang, and Huan Liu. 2015. User identification across social media. *ACM Transactions on Knowledge Discovery from Data (TKDD)*, 10(2).

Character-based Neural Embeddings for Tweet Clustering

Svitlana Vakulenko
Vienna University of Economics and Business, MODUL Technology GmbH
svitlana.vakulenko@wu.ac.at

Lyndon Nixon
MODUL Technology GmbH
nixon@modultech.eu

Mihai Lupu
TU Wien
Vienna, Austria
mihai.lupu@tuwien.ac.at

Abstract

In this paper we show how the performance of tweet clustering can be improved by leveraging character-based neural networks. The proposed approach overcomes the limitations related to the vocabulary explosion in the word-based models and allows for the seamless processing of the multilingual content. Our evaluation results and code are available on-line[1].

1 Introduction

Our use case scenario, as part of the InVID project[2], originates from the needs of professional journalists responsible for reporting breaking news in a timely manner. News often appear on social media exclusively or right before they appear in the traditional news media. Social media is also responsible for the rapid propagation of inaccurate or incomplete information (rumors). Therefore, it is important to provide efficient tools to enable journalists rapidly detect breaking news in social media streams (Petrovic et al., 2013).

The SNOW 2014 Data Challenge provided the task of extracting newsworthy topics from Twitter. The results of the challenge confirmed that the task is ambitious: The best result was 0.4 F-measure.

Breaking-news detection involves 3 subtasks: selection, clustering, and ranking of tweets. In this paper, we address the task of tweet clustering as one of the pivotal subtasks required to enable effective breaking news detection from Twitter.

Traditional approaches to clustering textual documents involve construction of a document-term matrix, which represents each document as a bag-of-words. These approaches also require language-specific sentence and word tokenization.

Word-based approaches fall short when applied to social media data, e.g., Twitter, where a lot of infrequent or misspelled words occur within very short documents. Hence, the document representation matrix becomes increasingly sparse.

One way to overcome sparseness in a tweet-term matrix is to consider only the terms that appear frequently across the collection and drop all the infrequent terms. This procedure effectively removes a considerable amount of information content. As a result, all tweets that do not contain any of the frequent terms receive a null-vector representation. These tweets are further ignored by the model and cannot influence clustering outcomes in the subsequent time intervals, where the frequency distribution may change, which hinders the detection of emerging topics.

Artificial neural networks (ANNs) allow to generate dense vector representation (embeddings), which can be efficiently generated on the word- as well as character levels (dos Santos and Zadrozny, 2014; Zhang et al., 2015; Dhingra et al., 2016). The main advantage of the character-based approaches is their language-independence, since they do not require any language-specific parsing.

The major contribution of our work is the evaluation of the character-based neural embeddings on the tweet clustering task. We show how to employ character-based tweet embeddings for the task of tweet clustering and demonstrate in the experimental evaluation that the proposed approach significantly outperforms the current state-of-the-art in tweet clustering for breaking news detection.

The remaining of this paper is structured as follows: Section 2 provides an overview of the related work; we describe the setup of an extensive evaluation in Section 3; report and discuss the results in Sections 4 and 5, respectively; conclu-

[1] https://github.com/vendi12/tweet2vec_clustering

[2] http://www.invid-project.eu

Proceedings of the Fifth International Workshop on Natural Language Processing for Social Media , pages 36–44,
Valencia, Spain, April 3-7, 2017. ©2017 Association for Computational Linguistics

sion (Section 6) summarizes our findings and directions for future work.

2 Related Work

2.1 Breaking news detection

There has been a continuous effort over the recent years to design effective and efficient algorithms capable of detecting newsworthy topics in the Twitter stream (Hayashi et al., 2015; Ifrim et al., 2014; Vosecky et al., 2013; Wurzer et al., 2015). These current state-of-the-art approaches build upon the bag-of-words document model, which results in high-dimensional, sparse representations that do not scale well and are not aware of semantic similarities, such as paraphrases.

The problem becomes evident in case of tweets that contain short texts with a long tail of infrequent slang and misspelled words. The performance of the such approaches over Twitter datasets is very low, with F-measure up to 0.2 against the annotated Wikipidea articles as reference topics (Wurzer et al., 2015) and 0.4 against the curated topic pool (Papadopoulos et al., 2014).

2.2 Neural embeddings

Artificial neural networks (ANNs) allow to generate dense vector representations (embeddings). Word2vec (Mikolov et al., 2013) is by far the most popular approach. It accumulates the cooccurrence statistics of words that efficiently summarizes their semantics.

Brigadir et al. (2014) demonstrated encouraging results using the word2vec Skip-gram model to generate event timelines from tweets. Moran et al. (2016) achieved an improvement over the state-of-the-art first story detection (FSD) results by expanding the tweets with their semantically related terms using word2vec.

Neural embeddings can be efficiently generated on the character level as well. They repeatedly outperformed the word-level baselines on the tasks of language modeling (Kim et al., 2016), part-of-speech tagging (dos Santos and Zadrozny, 2014), and text classification (Zhang et al., 2015). The main advantage of the character-based approach is its language-independence, since it does not depend on any language-specific preprocessing.

Dhingra et al. (2016) proposed training a recurrent neural network on the task of hashtag prediction. Vosoughi et al. (2016) demonstrated an improved performance of a character-based neural autoencoder on the task of paraphrase and semantic similarity detection in tweets.

Our work extends the evaluation of the Tweet2Vec model (Dhingra et al., 2016) to the tweet clustering task, versus the traditional document-term matrix representation. To the best of our knowledge, this work is the first attempt to evaluate the performance of character-based neural embeddings on the tweet clustering task.

3 Experimental Evaluation

3.1 Dataset

Description and preprocessing. We use the SNOW 2014 test dataset (Papadopoulos et al., 2014) in our evaluation. It contains the IDs of about 1 million tweets produced within 24 hours.

We retrieved 845,626 tweets from the Twitter API, since other tweets had already been deleted from the platform. The preprocessing procedure: remove RT prefixes, urls and user mentions, bring all characters to lower case and separate punctuation with spaces (the later is necessary only for the word-level baseline).

The dataset is further separated into 5 subsets corresponding to the 1-hour time intervals (18:00, 22:00, 23:15, 01:00 and 01:30) that are annotated with the list of breaking news topics. In total, we have 48,399 tweets for clustering evaluation; the majority of them (42,758 tweets) are in English.

The dataset comes with the list of the breaking news topics. These topics were manually selected by the independent evaluators from the topic pool collected from all challenge participants (external topics). The list of topics contains 70 breaking news headlines extracted from tweets (e.g., "The new, full Godzilla trailer has roared online"). Each topic is annotated with a few (at most 4) tweet IDs, which is not sufficient for an adequate evaluation of a tweet clustering algorithm.

Dataset extension. We enrich the topic annotations by collecting larger tweet clusters using fuzzy string matching[3] for each of the topic labels. Fuzzy string matching uses the Levenstein (edit) distance (Levenshtein, 1966) between the two input strings as the measure of similarity. Levenstein distance corresponds to the minimum number of character edits (insertions, deletions, or substitutions) required to transform one string into the

[3] `https://github.com/seatgeek/fuzzywuzzy`

other. We choose only the tweets for which the similarity ratio with the topic string is greater than 0.9 threshold.

A sample tweet cluster produced with the fuzzy string matching for the topic "Justin Trudeau apologizes for Ukraine joke":

- Justin Trudeau apologizes for *Ukraine joke*: Justin Trudeau said he's spoken the head...
- Justin Trudeau apologizes for *Ukraine comments* `http://t.co/7ImWTRONXt`
- Justin Trudeau apologizes for *Ukraine hockey joke* #cdnpoli

In total, we matched 2,585 tweets to 132 clusters using this approach. The resulting tweet clusters represent the ground-truth topics within different time intervals. The cluster size varies from 1 to 361 tweets with an average of 20 tweets per cluster (median: 6.5).

This simple procedure allows us to automatically generate high-quality partial labeling. We further use this topic assignment as the ground-truth class labels to automatically evaluate different flat clustering partitions.

3.2 Tweet representation approaches

TweetTerm. Our baseline is the tweet representation approach that was used in the winner-system of SNOW 2014 Data Challenge[4] (Ifrim et al., 2014). This approach represents a collection of tweets as a tweet-term matrix by keeping the bigrams and trigrams that occur at least in 10 tweets.

Tweet2Vec. This approach includes two stages: (1) *training* a neural network to predict hashtags using the subset of tweets that contain hashtags (88,148 tweets in our case); (2) *encoding*: use the trained model to produce tweet embeddings for all the tweets regardless whether they contain hashtags or not. We use Tweet2Vec implementation[5] to produce tweet embeddings.

Tweet2Vec is a bi-directional recurrent neural network that consumes textual input as a sequence of characters. The network architecture includes two Gated Recurrent Units (GRUs) (Cho et al., 2014): forward and backward GRUs. GRU is an optimized version of a Long Short-Term Memory (LSTM) architecture (Hochreiter and Schmidhuber, 1997). It includes 2 gates that control the information flow. The gates (reset and update gate) regulate how much the previous output state (h_{t-1}) influences the current state (h_t).

The two GRUs are identical, but the backward GRU receives the same sequence of tweet-characters in reverse order. Each GRU computes its own vector-representation for every substring (h_t) using the current character vector (x_t) and the vector-representation it computed a step before (h_{t-1}). These two representations of the same tweet are combined in the next layer of the neural network to produce the final tweet embedding (see more details in Dhingra et.al. (2016)).

The network is trained in minibatches with an objective function to predict the previously removed hashtags. A hashtag can be considered as the ground-truth cluster label for tweets. Therefore, the network is trained to optimize for the correct tweet classification, which corresponds to a supervised version of the tweet clustering task annotated with the cluster assignment, i.e. hashtags.

In order to predict the hashtags the tweet embeddings are passed through the linear layer, which produces the output in the size of the number of hashtags, which we observed in the training dataset. The softmax layer on top normalizes the scores from the linear layer to generate the hashtag probabilities for every input tweet.

Tweet embeddings are produced by passing the tweets through the trained Tweet2Vec model (encoder). In this way we can obtain vector representations for all the tweets including the ones that do not contain any hashtags. The result is a matrix of size $n \times h$, where n is the number of tweets and h is the number of hidden states (500).

3.3 Clustering

To cluster tweet vectors (character-based tweet embeddings produced by the neural network for Tweet2Vec evaluation or the document-term matrix for TweetTerm) we employ the hierarchical clustering algorithm implementation from *fastcluster* library (Müllner, 2013).

Hierarchical clustering includes computing pairwise distances between the tweet vectors, followed by their linkage into a single dendrogram. There are several distance metrics (Euclidean, Manhattan, cosine, etc.) and linkage methods to compare distances (single, average, complete, weighted, etc.). We evaluated the performance of different methods using the cophenetic correlation

[4] `https://github.com/heerme/twitter-topics`

[5] `https://github.com/bdhingra/tweet2vec`

coefficient (CPCC) (Sokal and Rohlf, 1962) and found the best performing combination: Euclidean distance and average linkage method.

The hierarchical clustering dendrogram can produce n different flat clusterings for the same dataset: from n single-member clusters with one document per cluster to a single cluster that contains all n documents. The distance threshold defines the granularity (number and size) of the produced clusters.

3.4 Distance threshold selection

Grid search helps us to determine the optimal distance threshold for the dendrogram cut-off. We generated a list of values in the range from 0.1 to 1.5 with 0.1 increment step and examine their performance with respect to the ground-truth cluster assignment. We produce flat clusterings for each value of the distance threshold from the grid and compare them with respect to the quality metrics.

Since we also want to be able to select the optimal distance threshold in absence of the true labels, we examine the scores provided by the mean Silhouette coefficient (Rousseeuw, 1987). Silhouette is an unsupervised intrinsic evaluation metric (cluster validity index) that measures the quality of the produced clusters and can be used for unsupervised intrinsic evaluation (i.e., without the ground-truth labels). It was reported to outperform alternative methods in a comparative study of 30 validity indices (Arbelaitz et al., 2013).

3.5 Clustering Evaluation Metrics

We evaluate the clustering results using the standard metrics for extrinsic clustering evaluation: homogeneity, completeness, V-Measure (Rosenberg and Hirschberg, 2007), Adjusted Rand Index (ARI) (Hubert and Arabie, 1985) and Adjusted Mutual Information (AMI) (Nguyen et al., 2010). All metrics return a score on the range [0; 1] for the pair of sets that contain ground truth and cluster labels as input. The higher the score the more similar the two clusterings are.

The **Homogeneity** score represents the measure for purity of the produced clusters. It penalizes clustering, where members of different classes get clustered together. Thus, the best homogeneity scores are always at the bottom of the dendrogram, i.e., at the level of the leaves, where each document belongs to its own cluster. **Completeness**, on the contrary, favors larger clusters and reduces the score if the members of the same class are split into different clusters. Therefore, the top of the dendrogram, where all the documents reside in a single cluster always achieves the maximum completeness score.

V-Measure is designed to balance out the two extremes of homogeneity and completeness. It is the harmonic mean of the two and corresponds to the Normalized Mutual Information (NMI) score.

AMI score is an extension of NMI adjusted for chance. The more clusters are considered the more chance the labelings correlate. AMI allows us to compare the clustering performance across different time intervals since it normalizes the score by the number of labeled clusters in each interval.

Finally, **ARI** is an alternative way to assess the agreement between two clusterings. It counts all pairs clustered together or separated in different clusters. ARI also accounts for the chance of an overlap in a random label assignment.

3.6 Manual Cluster Evaluation

Our partial labeling covers a small subset of the data and by design provides the clusters with the high degree of string overlap with the annotated topics. Therefore, we extend the clustering evaluation to the rest of the dataset to evaluate whether the models can uncover less straight-forward semantic similarities in tweets. We select the results for manual evaluation motivated by the cluster label (headline) selection task.

The next step in the breaking news detection pipeline after the clustering task is headline selection (cluster labeling task). The most common approach to label a cluster of tweets is to select a single tweet as a representative member for the whole cluster (Papadopoulos et al., 2014). We decided to test this assumption and manually check how many clusters loose their semantics when represented with a single tweet.

Headline selection motivates the coherence assessment of the produced clusters since the clusters discarded at this stage will never make it to the final results. To explore coherence of the produced clusters we pick several tweets in each cluster and check whether they are semantically similar.

The tweet selected as a headline (cluster label) can be the first published tweet as in First Story Detection (FSD) task, also used in Ifrim et al (2014). Alternative approaches include selection of the most recent tweet published on the topic, or the tweet that is semantically most similar

Interval	Tweets	Model	Dimensions	Distance threshold	Clusters	Homogeneity	Completeness	V-Measure	ARI	AMI
18:00	10,344	Tweet2Vec	500	1	3026	**0.9958**	0.9453	**0.9699**	**0.9804**	**0.9376**
		TweetTerm	433	1-1.3	66-79	0.9277	**1**	0.9625	0.949	0.9216
22:00	14,471	Tweet2Vec	500	0.9	5292	**1**	0.9601	**0.9796**	**0.9922**	**0.9571**
		TweetTerm	589	0.7-1.3	93-118	0.9385	**0.9969**	0.9668	0.9859	0.9359
23:15	8,231	Tweet2Vec	500	0.8	3986	**1**	0.98	**0.9899**	**0.9948**	**0.9743**
		TweetTerm	565	0.01-1.3	67-142	0.8062	**0.9978**	0.8918	0.7344	0.7763
01:00	5,123	Tweet2Vec	500	0.9	2242	**1**	0.8877	**0.9405**	**0.8668**	**0.8327**
		TweetTerm	721	0.8-1.3	71-111	0.8104	**1**	0.8953	0.8188	0.7666
01:30	4,589	Tweet2Vec	500	0.9	2091	**1**	0.8762	**0.934**	**0.8089**	**0.8129**
		TweetTerm	635	1.2-1.3	64-78	0.8024	**1**	0.8903	0.7809	0.754

Table 1: Results of clustering evaluation on the English-language dataset

to all other tweets in the cluster, i.e., the tweet closest to the centroid of the cluster (**medoid-tweets**). Therefore, we sample 5 tweets from each cluster: the first published tweet, the most recent tweet and three medoid-tweets.

We set up a manual evaluation task as follows:

1. Take the top 20 largest clusters sorted by the number of tweets that belong to the cluster.
2. For each cluster:
   (a) Take the first and the last published tweet (tweets are previously sorted by the publication date).
   (b) Take three medoid-tweets, i.e., the tweets that appear closest to the centroid of the cluster.
   (c) Add the 5 tweets to the set associated with the cluster (removing exact duplicate tweets)
3. For all clusters, where the set of selected tweets contains at least two unique tweets: 4 human evaluators independently assess the coherence of each cluster.

According to the evaluation setup each model produced 20 top-clusters for each of the 5 intervals, i.e., $20 \times 5 = 100$ clusters per model. We manually evaluate only the clusters that contain more than 1 distinct representative tweet (**Clusters>1**). All other clusters, i.e., the ones for which all 5 selected tweets are identical (**Clusters=1**), are considered correct by default.

Results for all 5 intervals were evaluated together in a single pool and the models were anonymized to avoid biases. Each evaluator independently assigned a single score to each cluster:

- **Correct** – all tweets report the same news;
- **Partial** – some tweets are not related;
- **Incorrect** – all tweets are not related.

Partial and Incorrect labels reflect different types of clustering errors. Partial error is less severe indicating that the tweets of the cluster are semantically similar, but they report different news (events) and should be split into several clusters. Incorrect clusters indicate a random collection of tweets with no semantic similarities.

4 Results

4.1 Results of Clustering Evaluation

Table 1 summarizes the results of our evaluation using the ground-truth partial labeling. The scores highlighted with the bold font indicate the best result among the two competing approaches for the same subset of tweets corresponding to the respective time interval.

Tweet2Vec exhibits better clustering performance comparing to the baseline according to the majority of the evaluation metrics in all the intervals. In all cases Tweet2Vec model wins in terms of Homogeneity score and TweetTerm wins in Completeness. This result shows that Tweet2Vec is better at separating tweets that are not similar enough than the baseline model. Tweet2Vec fails only once to perfectly separate the ground-truth clusters (18:00 interval). This result shows that Tweet2Vec is able to replicate the results of the fuzzy string matching algorithm that was used to generate the ground-truth labeling.

4.2 Results of Distance Threshold Selection

The rise in V-Measure correlates with the decline of the Silhouette coefficient and the steep drop in the number of produced clusters (see Figure 1). We observed that the optimal distance threshold for Tweet2Vec clustering according to V-Measure is on the interval [0.8; 1] (see Table 1: Distance threshold), which is also consistent with the findings reported in Ifrim et. al (2014).

Model	Dataset	Clusters	Correct (%)			Errors (%)	
			Clusters=1	Clusters>1	Total	Partial	Incorrect
Tweet2Vec	English	100	**80**	8.3	**88.3**	10	**1.8**
TweetTerm	English	95	71	**17.4**	87.9	8.9	3.2
Tweet2Vec	Multilingual	100	67	12.5	**79.5**	13	7.5

Table 2: Results of manual cluster evaluation. Note: the last row shows results on a different dataset and can not be directly compared with the other models.

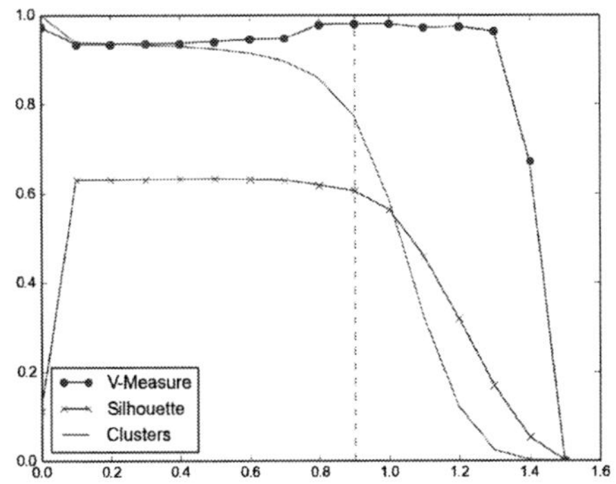

Figure 1: Correlation between the V-Measure, Silhouette coefficient and the number of clusters per tweet (Tweet2Vec 22:00 interval). The vertical red line indicates the maximum V-Measure score.

4.3 Results of Manual Cluster Evaluation

Results of the manual cluster evaluation by four independent evaluators are summarized in Table 2. Bold font indicates the maximum scores achieved across the competing representation approaches. Tables 3 and 4 show sample clusters produced by both models alongside their average score.

TweetTerm assigns a 0-vector representation to tweets that do not contain any of the frequent terms. Hence, all these tweets end up in a single "garbage" cluster. Therefore, we discount the number of the expected "garbage" clusters (1 cluster per interval = 5 clusters) from the score count for TweetTerm (Table 2).

Tweet2Vec model produces the largest number of perfectly homogeneous clusters for which all 5 selected tweets are identical (see Table 2 column Clusters=1). The percentage of correct results among the manually evaluated clusters is higher for the TweetTerm model, but the number of errors (Incorrect) is higher as well. Tweet2Vec produced the highest total % of correct clusters due to the larger proportion of detected clusters that contain identical tweets (Clusters=1). Tweet2Vec also produced the least number of incorrect clusters: at most 2 incorrect clusters per 100 clusters (Precision: 0.98).

The results of Tweet2Vec on the multilingual dataset are lower than on the English-language tweets. However, we do not have alternative results to compare since the baseline approach is not language-independent and requires additional functionality (word-level tokenizers) to handle tweets in other languages, e.g., Arabic or Chinese. We provide this evaluation results to demonstrate that Tweet2Vec overcomes this limitation and is able to cluster tweets in different languages. In particular, we obtained correct clusters of Russian and Arabic tweets.

We observed that leaving the urls does not significantly affect clustering performance, i.e., the model tolerates noise. However, replacement of the urls and user mentions with placeholders as in Dhingra et. al. (2016) generates syntactic patterns in text, such as @user @user @user, which causes semantically unrelated tweets appear within the same cluster.

5 Discussion

Our experimental evaluation showed that the character-based embeddings produced with a neural network outperform the document-term baseline on the tweet clustering task. The baseline approach (TweetTerm) shows a very good performance in comparison with the simplicity of its implementation, but it naturally falls short in recognizing patterns beyond simple n-gram matching.

We attribute this result to the inherent limitation of the document-term model retaining only the frequent terms and disregarding the long tail of infrequent patterns. This limitation appears crucial in the task of emergent news detection, in which the topics need to be detected long before they become popular. Neural embeddings, in contrast, can retain a sufficient level of detail in their representa-

Sample Cluster	Evaluation
video : **bitcoin : mtgox** exchange goes offline - **bitcoin** , a virtual currency ... the slow-motion collapse of **mt . gox** is **bitcoin**'s first financial crisis **:** now **bitcoin** users ... Disastro **bitcoin** : **mt . gox** cessa ogni attivite ... **: mt . gox** , il pi grande cambiavalute **bitco** ...	Correct
california couple finds time capsules **worth $10 million** **californian couple finds $10 million worth** of gold coins in tin can	Correct
ukraine puts off vote on new government despite eu pleas for quick action - washington post ... **ukraine** truce shattered , death toll hits 67 - kiev (reuters) - ukraine suffered its bloodiest day ... **ukraine** fighting leaves at least 18 dead as kiev barricades burn - clashes in ukraine ...	Partial
are you going to come on his network and get poor ratings too **?** **are you** sold on the waffle taco **?**	Incorrect
the chromecast app flood has started **by** **the** importance of emotion in design **by**	Incorrect

Table 3: Tweet2Vec sample results. Rows of the table show sample tweet clusters. Each line within the row corresponds to a separate tweet (after preprocessing, i.e. usernames and urls removed.)

Sample Cluster	Evaluation
obama : michelle and i were saddened to hear of the passing of **harold ramis**... touching tribute to ghostbusters star **harold ramis** from comic artist on the joyful comedy of **harold ramis**	Correct
major tokyo-based bitcoin exchange **mt . gox goes dark** "bitcoin exchange giant **mt . gox goes dark** — popular science "	Correct
obesity rate for young children plummets **43 %** in a **decade** the national **obesity rate for young children** dropped **43 %** over the past **decade**	Correct
diplomatic pressure is unlikely to reverse uganda's cruel **anti-gay** law provisions of arizona proposed **anti-gay** law even mitt romney wants arizona's governor to veto the state's **anti-gay** bill icymi : arizona pizzeria response to state **anti-gay** bill	Partial
amazing debate nic ! **well done** ! **well done** 4 -0 **well done** ! i find running so difficult . feel proud ! **well done** him :-) **well done** nicola my money is on you you done it well tonight ??	Incorrect

Table 4: TweetTerm sample results. Rows of the table show sample tweet clusters.

tions and are able to mirror the fuzzy string matching performance beyond simple n-gram matching.

It becomes apparent from the sample clustering results (Tables 3 and 4) that both models perform essentially the same task of unveiling patterns shared between a group of strings. While TweetTerm operates only on the patterns of identical n-grams, Tweet2Vec goes beyond this limitation by providing room for a variation within the n-gram substring similar to fuzzy string matching. This effect allows to capture subtle variations in strings, e.g., misspellings, which word-based approaches are incapable of.

Our error analysis also revealed the limitation of the neural embeddings to distinguish between semantic and syntactic similarity in strings (see Incorrect samples in Table 3). Tweet2Vec, as a recurrent neural network approach, represents not only the characters but also their order in string that may be a false similarity signal. It is evident that the neural representations in our example would benefit from the stop-word removal or an analogous to TF/IDF weighting scheme to avoid capturing punctuation and other merely syntactic patterns.

Limitations. Neural networks gain performance when more data is available. We could use only 88,148 tweets from the dataset to train the neural network, which can appear insufficient to unfold the potential of the model to recognize more complex patterns. Also, due to the scarce annotation available we could use only a small subset of the original dataset for our clustering evaluation. Since most of the SNOW tweets are in English, another dataset is needed for comprehensive multilingual clustering evaluation.

6 Conclusion

We showed that character-based neural embeddings enable accurate tweet clustering with minimum supervision. They provide fine-grained representations that can help to uncover fuzzy similarities in strings beyond simple n-gram matching. We also demonstrated the limitation of the current approach unable to distinguish semantic from syntactic patterns in strings, which provides a clear direction for the future work.

7 Acknowledgments

The presented work was supported by the InVID Project (http://www.invid-project.eu/), funded by the European Union's Horizon 2020 research and innovation programme under grant agreement No 687786. Mihai Lupu was supported by Self-Optimizer (FFG 852624) in the EUROSTARS programme, funded by EUREKA, the BMWFW and the European Union, and ADMIRE (P25905-N23) by FWF. We thank to Bhuwan Dhingra for the support in using Tweet2Vec and Linda Andersson for the review and helpful comments.

References

Olatz Arbelaitz, Ibai Gurrutxaga, Javier Muguerza, Jesús M. Pérez, and Iñigo Perona. 2013. An extensive comparative study of cluster validity indices. *Pattern Recognition*, 46(1):243–256.

Igor Brigadir, Derek Greene, and Padraig Cunningham. 2014. Adaptive Representations for Tracking Breaking News on Twitter. In *NewsKDD - Workshop on Data Science for News Publishing at The 20th ACM SIGKDD International Conference on Knowledge Discovery and Data Mining, KDD '14, August 24-27, 2014, New York, NY, USA*.

Kyunghyun Cho, Bart van Merrienboer, Çaglar Gülçehre, Dzmitry Bahdanau, Fethi Bougares, Holger Schwenk, and Yoshua Bengio. 2014. Learning phrase representations using RNN encoder-decoder for statistical machine translation. In *Proceedings of the 2014 Conference on Empirical Methods in Natural Language Processing, EMNLP 2014, October 25-29, 2014, Doha, Qatar*, pages 1724–1734.

Bhuwan Dhingra, Zhong Zhou, Dylan Fitzpatrick, Michael Muehl, and William W. Cohen. 2016. Tweet2vec: Character-based distributed representations for social media. In *Proceedings of the 54th Annual Meeting of the Association for Computational Linguistics, ACL 2016, August 7-12, 2016, Berlin, Germany*.

Cícero Nogueira dos Santos and Bianca Zadrozny. 2014. Learning character-level representations for part-of-speech tagging. In *Proceedings of the 31th International Conference on Machine Learning, ICML 2014, 21-26 June, 2014, Beijing, China*, pages 1818–1826.

Kohei Hayashi, Takanori Maehara, Masashi Toyoda, and Ken-ichi Kawarabayashi. 2015. Real-Time Top-R Topic Detection on Twitter with Topic Hijack Filtering. In *Proceedings of the 21th ACM SIGKDD International Conference on Knowledge Discovery and Data Mining, August 10-13, 2015, Sydney, Australia*, pages 417–426.

Sepp Hochreiter and Jürgen Schmidhuber. 1997. Long short-term memory. *Neural Computation*, 9(8):1735–1780.

Lawrence Hubert and Phipps Arabie. 1985. Comparing partitions. *Journal of classification*, 2(1):193–218.

Georgiana Ifrim, Bichen Shi, and Igor Brigadir. 2014. Event Detection in Twitter using Aggressive Filtering and Hierarchical Tweet Clustering. In Symeon Papadopoulos, David Corney, and Luca Maria Aiello, editors, *Proceedings of the SNOW 2014 Data Challenge co-located with 23rd International World Wide Web Conference (WWW 2014), April 8, 2014, Seoul, Korea*, pages 33–40.

Yoon Kim, Yacine Jernite, David Sontag, and Alexander M. Rush. 2016. Character-aware neural language models. In *Proceedings of the Thirtieth AAAI Conference on Artificial Intelligence, February 12-17, 2016, Phoenix, Arizona, USA*, pages 2741–2749.

Vladimir I. Levenshtein. 1966. Binary codes capable of correcting deletions, insertions and reversals. In *Soviet physics doklady*, volume 10, page 707.

Tomas Mikolov, Ilya Sutskever, Kai Chen, Gregory S. Corrado, and Jeffrey Dean. 2013. Distributed Representations of Words and Phrases and their Compositionality. In Christopher J. C. Burges, Lon Bottou, Zoubin Ghahramani, and Kilian Q. Weinberger, editors, *Advances in Neural Information Processing Systems 26: 27th Annual Conference on Neural Information Processing Systems 2013. Proceedings of a meeting held December 5-8, 2013, Lake Tahoe, Nevada, United States*, pages 3111–3119.

Sean Moran, Richard McCreadie, Craig Macdonald, and Iadh Ounis. 2016. Enhancing First Story Detection using Word Embeddings. In *Proceedings of the 39th International ACM SIGIR conference on Research and Development in Information Retrieval, SIGIR 2016, July 17-21, 2016, Pisa, Italy*, pages 821–824.

Daniel Müllner. 2013. fastcluster: Fast hierarchical, agglomerative clustering routines for r and python. *Journal of Statistical Software*, 53(1):1–18.

Xuan Vinh Nguyen, Julien Epps, and James Bailey. 2010. Information theoretic measures for clusterings comparison: Variants, properties, normalization and correction for chance. *Journal of Machine Learning Research*, 11:2837–2854.

Symeon Papadopoulos, David Corney, and Luca Maria Aiello. 2014. SNOW 2014 Data Challenge: Assessing the Performance of News Topic Detection Methods in Social Media. In Symeon Papadopoulos, David Corney, and Luca Maria Aiello, editors,

Proceedings of the SNOW 2014 Data Challenge co-located with 23rd International World Wide Web Conference (WWW 2014), April 8, 2014, Seoul, Korea, pages 1–8.

Sasa Petrovic, Miles Osborne, Richard McCreadie, Craig Macdonald, Iadh Ounis, and Luke Shrimpton. 2013. Can twitter replace newswire for breaking news? In Emre Kiciman, Nicole B. Ellison, Bernie Hogan, Paul Resnick, and Ian Soboroff, editors, *Proceedings of the Seventh International Conference on Weblogs and Social Media, ICWSM 2013, July 8-11, 2013, Cambridge, Massachusetts, USA*.

Andrew Rosenberg and Julia Hirschberg. 2007. V-measure: A conditional entropy-based external cluster evaluation measure. In *EMNLP-CoNLL 2007, Proceedings of the 2007 Joint Conference on Empirical Methods in Natural Language Processing and Computational Natural Language Learning, June 28-30, 2007, Prague, Czech Republic*, pages 410–420.

Peter J. Rousseeuw. 1987. Silhouettes: A graphical aid to the interpretation and validation of cluster analysis. *Journal of Computational and Applied Mathematics*, 20:53 – 65.

Robert R. Sokal and F. James Rohlf. 1962. The comparison of dendrograms by objective methods. *Taxon*, 11(2):33–40.

Jan Vosecky, Di Jiang, Kenneth Wai-Ting Leung, and Wilfred Ng. 2013. Dynamic multi-faceted topic discovery in twitter. In *22nd ACM International Conference on Information and Knowledge Management, CIKM'13, October 27 - November 1, 2013, San Francisco, CA, USA*, pages 879–884.

Soroush Vosoughi, Prashanth Vijayaraghavan, and Deb Roy. 2016. Tweet2vec: Learning tweet embeddings using character-level CNN-LSTM encoder-decoder. In *Proceedings of the 39th International ACM SIGIR conference on Research and Development in Information Retrieval, SIGIR 2016, July 17-21, 2016, Pisa, Italy*, pages 1041–1044.

Dominik Wurzer, Victor Lavrenko, and Miles Osborne. 2015. Tracking unbounded Topic Streams. In *Proceedings of the 53rd Annual Meeting of the Association for Computational Linguistics and the 7th International Joint Conference on Natural Language Processing of the Asian Federation of Natural Language Processing, ACL 2015, July 26-31, 2015, Beijing, China*, pages 1765–1773.

Xiang Zhang, Junbo Zhao, and Yann LeCun. 2015. Character-level convolutional networks for text classification. In *Advances in Neural Information Processing Systems 28: Annual Conference on Neural Information Processing Systems 2015, December 7-12, 2015, Montreal, Quebec, Canada*, pages 649–657.

A Twitter Corpus and Benchmark Resources for German Sentiment Analysis

Mark Cieliebak
SpinningBytes
mc@spinningbytes.com

Jan Deriu
Zurich University of Applied Sciences
deri@zhaw.ch

Dominic Egger
Zurich University of Applied Sciences
eggo@zhaw.ch

Fatih Uzdilli
Zurich University of Applied Sciences
uzdi@zhaw.ch

Abstract

In this paper we present SB10k, a new corpus for sentiment analysis with approx. 10,000 German tweets.
We use this new corpus and two existing corpora to provide state-of-the-art benchmarks for sentiment analysis in German: we implemented a CNN (based on the winning system of SemEval-2016) and a feature-based SVM and compare their performance on all three corpora.
For the CNN, we also created German word embeddings trained on 300M tweets. These word embeddings were then optimized for sentiment analysis using distant-supervised learning.
The new corpus, the German word embeddings (plain and optimized), and source code to re-run the benchmarks are publicly available.

1 Introduction

With the advance of deep learning in text analytics, many benchmarks for text analytics tasks have been significantly improved in the last four years. For this reason, Zurich University of Applied Sciences (ZHAW) and SpinningBytes AG are collaborating in a joint research project to develop state-of-the-art solutions for text analytics tasks in several European languages. The goal is to adapt and optimize algorithms for tasks like sentiment analysis, named entity recognition (NER), topic extraction etc. into industry-ready software libraries.

One very challenging task is automatic sentiment analysis. The goal of sentiment analysis is to classify a text into the classes positive, negative, mixed, or neutral. Interest in automatic sentiment analysis has recently increased in both academia and industry due to the huge number of documents which are publicly available on social media. In fact, there exist various initiatives in the scientific community (such as shared tasks at SemEval (Nakov et al., 2016) or TREC (Ounis et al., 2008)), competitions at Kaggle[1], special tracks at major conferences like EMNLP or LREC, and several companies have built commercial sentiment analysis tools (Cieliebak et al., 2013).

Deep learning for sentiment analysis. Deep neural networks have become very successful for sentiment analysis. In fact, the winner and many top-ranked systems in SemEval-2016 were using deep neural networks (SemEval is an international competition that runs every year several tasks for semantic evaluation, including sentiment analysis) (Nakov et al., 2016). The winning system uses a multi-layer convolutional neural network that is trained in three phases. For English, this system achieves an F1-score of 62.7% on the test data of SemEval-2016 (Deriu et al., 2016), and top scores on test data from previous years. For this reason, we decided to adapt the system for sentiment analysis in German. Details are described in Section 4.

A new corpus for German sentiment. In order to train the CNN, millions of unlabeled and weakly-labeled German tweets are used for creating the word embeddings. In addition, a sufficient amount of manually labeled tweets is required to train and optimize the system. For languages such as English, Chinese or Arabic, there exist plenty of labeled training data for sentiment analysis, while for other European languages, the resources are often very limited (cf. "Related Work"). For German, in particular, we are only aware of three sentiment corpora of significant size: the DAI tweet data set, which contains 1800 German tweets with tweet-level sentiments (Narr et al., 2012); the

[1] https://www.kaggle.com/c/sentiment-analysis-on-movie-reviews

Proceedings of the Fifth International Workshop on Natural Language Processing for Social Media , pages 45–51,
Valencia, Spain, April 3-7, 2017. ©2017 Association for Computational Linguistics

MGS corpus, which contains 109,130 German tweets (Mozetič et al., 2016); and the PotTS corpus, which contains 7992 German tweets that were annotated on phrase level (Sidarenka, 2016). Unfortunately, the first corpus is too small for training a sentiment system, the the second corpus has a very low inter-annotator agreement ($\alpha = 0.34$), indicating low-quality annotations, and the third corpus is not on sentence level.

For this reason, we decided to construct a large sentiment corpus with German tweets, called *SB10k*. This corpus should allow to train high-quality machine learning classifiers. It contains 9783 German tweets, each labeled by three annotators. Details of corpus construction and properties are described in Section 3.

Benchmark for German Sentiment. We evaluate the performance of the CNN on the three German sentiment corpora CAI, MGS, and SB10k in Section 5. In addition, we compare the results to a baseline system, a feature-based Support Vector Machine (SVM). To our knowledge, this is the first large-scale benchmark for sentiment analysis on German tweets.

Main Contributions. Our main contributions are:

- Benchmarks for sentiment analysis in German on three corpora.
- A new corpus *SB10k* for German sentiment with approx. 10000 tweets, manually labeled by three annotators.
- Publicly available word embeddings trained on 300M million German tweets (using word2vec), and modified word embeddings after distant-supervised learning with 40M million weakly-labeled sentiment tweets.

The new corpus, word embeddings for German (plain and fully-trained) and source code to re-run the benchmarks are available at `www.spinningbytes.com/resources`.

2 Related Work

There exists a tremendous amount of literature on sentiment analysis in general; for a good introduction and overview, see the recent book by Bing Liu (Zhao et al., 2016).

Corpora. Several human labeled corpora for sentiment analysis are available, which differ in: languages they cover, size, annotation schemes (number of annotators, sentiment), and document domains (tweets, news, blogs, product reviews etc.). For English there exist various corpora, e.g. for tweets (Narr et al., 2012), product reviews (Hu and Liu, 2004) or news (Wiebe et al., 2005), and sentiment corpora exist also for other European languges such as Italian (Straniscim et al., 2016), French (Bosco et al., 2016), Spanish (Martinez-Camara et al., 2016; Martinez-Camara et al., 2015) or Dutch (Verhoeven and Daelemans, 2014).

Sentiment Analysis in German. German is the most-spoken native language in Europe[2], and several research activities and events are focussed on German sentiment analysis. The Interest Group on German Sentiment Analysis (IGGSA)is a European collaboration of researchers working on German sentiment analysis. Among other things, they hosted several workshops and shared tasks on German Sentiment analysis, e.g. GESTALT-2014 (Ruppenhofer et al., 2014). For an extended list of publications on sentiment analysis in German, we refer the reader to IGGSA[3] .

Machine Learning for Sentiment Analysis. Until recently, feature-based systems were frequently used for sentiment analysis. In fact, almost all systems participating in SemEval-2014 were feature-based, with SVM, MaxEnt, and Naive Bayes being the most popular classifiers in the competition (Rosenthal et al., 2014). However, neural networks have shown great promise in NLP over the past few years. Examples are in semantic analysis (Shen et al., 2014), machine translation (Gao et al., 2014) and sentiment analysis (Socher et al., 2013). In particular, shallow convolutional neural networks (CNNs) have recently improved the state-of-the-art in text polarity classification demonstrating a significant increase in terms of accuracy compared to previous state-of-the-art techniques (Kim, 2014; Kalchbrenner et al., 2014; dos Santos and Gatti, 2014; Severyn and Moschitti, 2015; Johnson and Zhang, 2015; Rothe et al., 2016; Deriu et al., 2017).

[2]www.languageknowledge.eu

[3]https://sites.google.com/site/iggsahome/

3 Corpus Construction

3.1 Goals

We constructed a new sentiment corpus with German tweets, called *SB10k*. This corpus should allow to train high-quality machine learning classifiers. Based on our experiences with machine learning in other languages, we aimed at the following goals:

- The corpus should contain 10000 tweets, to provide sufficient data for complex system to be trained
- Selected tweets should cover a wide variety of unigrams and topics
- Each tweet should be labeled by three expert annotators
- Sentiment labels should be as balanced as possible

3.2 Basic Data Set

Our initial data was made up of tweets collected between 01.08.2013 and 31.10.2013. Those tweets were a random subselection (10%) of all tweets published during that time span. With the langid.py tool (Lui and Baldwin, 2012) we selected all German tweets from within our initial data. To minimize false positives, we only included tweets with a German confidence score of over 0.999. This resulted in 5.280.157 tweets.

3.3 Tweet Selection

Next we selected the tweets to be annotated. In order to achieve a large variety of topic and unigrams that are covered by the corpus, we applied a k-means clustering with bag of words features and cosine similarity to create 2500 clusters of tweets. Our goal was to have - at the end - four tweets per cluster, one for each sentiment class.

The majority of tweets in Twitter do not contain any opinion at all. Hence, selecting a random set of tweets for manual annotation would result in an unbalanced set, with a strong majority of neutral tweets. To find tweets with potentially different sentiments, we used a straight-forward approach: For each tweet we counted the number of positive and negative polarity words in per tweet, using the German polarity clues lexicon (Waltinger, 2010). Using these polarity words as indicators, we selected tweets that were "probably" positive, negative, mixed, or neutral: A tweet was considered "probably positive" if it contained at least one positive polarity words, but no negative polarity words; "probably negative" analogously; "probably mixed" if both types of polarity words occured; and "probably neutral" if no polarity words occured. In order to reach an as balanced corpus as possible and increase the number of tweets with an opinion, we decided to use primarily probably mixed tweets, since they tended to be anything but neutral. Obviously, this approach lessened the number of observed unigrams and topics to some degree.

3.4 Manual Annotation

We had 34 annotators (students in computer science or linguistics). Every tweet was shown to 3 random annotators and labeled with a sentiment class by each of those. They were given several examples and instructed to "categorize the sentiment expressed in a tweet, not the sentiment felt when reading the tweet". We added a non-German flag to clean out tweets wich slipped by the language identification, and tweets were marked as "unknown" when annotators could not decide on its sentiment.

3.5 Corpus Properties

Basic Outline. The corpus *SB10k* contains 9783 German tweets. Each tweet has sentiment annotations on tweet level by 3 human annotators, using sentiment classes positive, negative, neutral, mixed, and unknown. We aggregate the annotators' individual classes to assign a sentiment to each tweet, where tweet t has sentiment S if at least 2 annotators marked the tweet with S; otherwise, sentiment of t is unknown. The distribution of aggregated annotations is shown in Table 1.

Pos.	Neg.	Neutral	Mixed	Unknown	**Total**
1682	1077	5266	330	1428	9738

Table 1: Number of tweets per sentiment in *SB10k*

Unigram Diversity. Goal of our clustering approach was to achieve a high diversity of unigrams in our corpus. We therefore compare the diversity of the tweets that were selected by our clustering versus randomly sampled tweets. There are $u = 11.592.947$ distinct unigrams in all collected German tweets (approx. 5 million). There are 9452 unigrams in the labeled tweets (picked from the k-means clustering), thus, the corpus covers 0.00081% of all unigrams. To compare this value to random sampling, we randomly picked 10000 tweets from all available tweets. This was repeated 10 times, resulting in an average coverage of 0.00075% of all unigrams. Thus, our clustering approach increases the number of encountered unigrams by 10.7%.

Annotator Agreement. To analyze the inter-annotator agreement within our corpus, we use Krippendorffs Alpha-reliability (Krippendorff, 2007). This agreement score fits well with our annotation scheme, in contrast to other scores like Kohens Kappa, since Krippendorffs Alpha basically computes the coincidence matrix between any two annotators, and calculates a weighed sum. We had pairs of annotators which shared as little as 1 tweet and pairs which shared as many as 1673 tweets. To mitigate this issue, we only considered pairs of annotators which shared at least 50 tweets. This results in $\alpha = 0.39$, with a standard deviation of 0.12.

4 Benchmark System: Multi-layer CNN with Three-Phase Training

4.1 Architecture and Implementation

The winning system of SemEval-2016 by team "SwissCheese" is based on a convolutional neural network (CNN) which is trained in three phases. We adapted and optimized the system for German sentiment analysis. In the following, we briefly describe the high-level architecture and parameters of this CNN. For more details on the network topology and technical architecture, see citederiu17www.

The core component of the system is a multi-layer convolutional neural network (CNN), which consists in two consecutive pairs of convolutional-pooling layers, followed by a single fully connected hidden layer and a soft-max output layer. The system is trained in three phases. Figure 1 shows a complete overview of the phases of the learning procedure: i) unsupervised phase, where word embeddings are created on a corpus of 300M unlabeled tweets; ii) distant supervised phase, where the network is trained on a weakly-labeled dataset of 40M tweets containing emoticons; and iii) supervised phase, where the network is nally trained on manually annotated tweets. For English, a similar system achieved an F1-score of 62.7% on the test data of SemEval-2016 (Deriu et al., 2016).

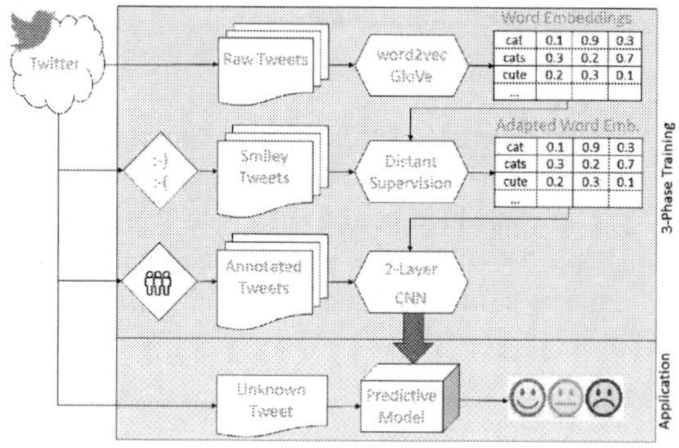

Figure 1: *Training Phases Overview.*

Training. The word embeddings are learned on an unsupervised corpus containing 300M German tweets. We apply a skip-gram model of window-size 5 and filter words that occur less than 15 times (Severyn and Moschitti, 2015). The dimensionality of the vector representation is set to $d = 52$. During the distant-supervised phase, we use emoticons to infer noisy labels on the tweets in the training set (Read, 2005; Go et al., 2009). We used 40M tweets (8M negative, 32M positive). The neural network was trained on these data for one epoch, before finally training on the supervised data for about 20 epochs. The word-embeddings are updated during both the distant- and the supervised training phases by applying back-propagation through the entire network.

Computing Time for Training. On a GPU computer with 3072 cores and 8GB of RAM, it took approximately 24 hours to create the word embeddings, 15 hours for the distant-supervised phase, and 30 minutes for the supervised phase.

5 Benchmark for German Sentiment Analysis

We now study how the CNN performs when trained and/or tested on the three German sentiment corpora we are aware of: *SB10k* (from this paper, 9738 tweets), *MGS* corpus (109'130 tweets, (Mozetič et al., 2016)), and *DAI* corpus (1800 tweets, (Narr et al., 2012)). Corpora *SB10k* and *MGS* were randomly split into training (90%) and

Classifier	Training Corpus	Test Corpus	$\mathbf{F1}_{pos}$	$\mathbf{F1}_{neg}$	$\mathbf{F1}_{neutral}$	**F1**
SVM	SB10k	SB10k	66.16	47.80	81.32	56.98
CNN	SB10k	SB10k	71.46	58.72	81.19	**65.09**
SVM	SB10k	MGS	49.50	38.62	66.41	44.06
CNN	SB10k	MGS	50.41	44.19	71.81	**47.30**
SVM	SB10k	DAI (full)	62.30	61.40	81.22	**61.85**
CNN	SB10k	DAI (full)	62.79	58.43	79.92	60.61
SVM	MGS	SB10k	67.77	53.23	80.20	60.50
CNN	MGS	SB10k	63.94	58.21	70.66	**61.07**
SVM	MGS	MGS	60.34	56.48	69.31	58.41
CNN	MGS	MGS	61.49	58.12	68.62	**59.80**
SVM	MGS	DAI (full)	59.32	56.03	74.83	57.68
CNN	MGS	DAI (full)	61.01	55.74	76.88	**58.38**

Table 2: Benchmarks for sentiment in German. SVM and CNN were trained on fixed split of each corpus (90%), and then tested on the remaining texts. For DAI, all texts were used for testing. F1 is macroaveraged from $F1_{pos}$ and $F1_{neg}$. Bold numbers identify higher F1 score of both classifiers for each combination of test and training corpus (2 lines).

testing (10%) subsets[4]. DAI was not split, since it was only used for testing.

For comparison, we implemented a feature-based system using a Support Vector Machine (SVM). Feature selection is based on the system described in (Uzdilli et al., 2015), which ranked 8th in the Semeval competition of 2015, and include n-gram, various lexical features, and statistical text properties. We use the macro-averages F1-score of positive and negative class, i.e. F1 = ($F1_{pos}$ + $F1_{neg}$) / 2, since this is also used in SemEval (Rosenthal et al., 2015) as a standard measure of quality. The results are reported in Table 2.

Results. We observe from Table 2 that CNN outperforms SVM in all but one case (SB10k-DAI). Surprisingly, SVM performs better on SB10k when trained on the foreign corpus MGS then when trained on SB10k (60.50 instead of 56.98), while in all other cases the classifier benefits when being trained on the same corpus. There is a high variance in F1-score for the same system on different test corpora, e.g. between 47.30 and 65.09 for CNN trained on SB10k.

Both SVM and CNN outperform the reference system from (Mozetič et al., 2016), which reported an F1-score of 53.6 for the German part of *MGS* (note that they used cross-validation instead of a fixed split of the corpus).

[4]These splits are available at `www.spinningbytes.com/resources` to allow other researchers to compare their results with the benchmarks

We also computed macroaveraged 3-class F1-score $F1_3$ = ($F1_{pos}$ + $F1_{neg}$ + $F1_{neutral}$) / 3, which is on average 4.42 points higher than F1, due to the higher values of $F1_{neutral}$.

6 Conclusion

We have evaluated two state-of-the-art systems for sentiment analysis in German on three Twitter corpora (on of them new). Since all corpora are publicly available, these results can serve as a benchmark for other sentiment systems in German.

The results show that the deep learning system outperforms the feature-based system in all but one cases. However, F1-score is around 60% in most cases, even when a system is trained and tested on the same corpus (with a fixed split of data). This means that there is still potential for inprovement.

7 Acknowledgements

This research has been funded by Commission for Technology and Innovation (CTI) project no. 18832.1 PFES-ES and by SpinningBytes AG, Switzerland. We would like to thank Leon Derczynski for giving us access to his tweet collection, and Matthias Flour for his support in labeling the tweets.

References

Cristina Bosco, Mirko Lai, Viviana Patti, and Daniela Virone. 2016. Tweeting and Being Ironic in the Debate about a Political Reform: the French Annotated Corpus TWitter-MariagePourTous. In *Proceedings of LREC-2016*, pages 1619–1626, Portoroz, Slovenia.

Mark Cieliebak, Oliver Dürr, and Fatih Uzdilli. 2013. Potential and Limitations of Commercial Sentiment Detection Tools. In *Proceedings of ESSEM@AI*IA*, pages 47–58, Torino, Italy.

Jan Deriu, Maurice Gonzenbach, Fatih Uzdilli, Aurelien Lucchi, Valeria De Luca, and Martin Jaggi. 2016. SwissCheese at SemEval-2016 Task 4: Sentiment classification using an ensemble of convolutional neural networks with distant supervision. In *Proceedings of SemEval-2016*, pages 1124–1128, San Diego, California, USA.

Jan Deriu, Aurelien Lucchi, Valeria De Luca, Aliaksei Severyn, Simon Müller, Mark Cieliebak, Thomas Hofmann, and Martin Jaggi. 2017. Leveraging large amounts of weakly supervised data for multi-language sentiment classification. In *Proceedings of WWW-2017*, Peth, Australia.

Cícero Nogueira dos Santos and Maira Gatti. 2014. Deep Convolutional Neural Networks for Sentiment Analysis of Short Texts. In *Proceedings of COLING-2014*, pages 69–78, Dublin, Ireland.

Jianfeng Gao, Xiaodong He, Wen-tau Yih, and Li Deng. 2014. Learning continuous phrase representations for translation modeling. In *Proceedings of ACL-2014*, pages 699–709, Baltimore, Maryland, USA.

Alec Go, Richa Bhayani, and Lei Huang. 2009. Twitter Sentiment Classification using Distant Supervision. Technical report, The Stanford Natural Language Processing Group, Stanford, CA, USA.

Minqing Hu and Bing Liu. 2004. Mining and summarizing customer reviews. In *Proceedings of ACM SIGKDD*, pages 168–177, Seattle, Washington, USA.

Rie Johnson and Tong Zhang. 2015. Semi-supervised Convolutional Neural Networks for Text Categorization via Region Embedding. In *Advances in Neural Information Processing Systems 28*, pages 919–927, Montreal, Canada.

Nal Kalchbrenner, Edward Grefenstette, and Phil Blunsom. 2014. A Convolutional Neural Network for Modelling Sentences. In *Proceedings of ACL-2014*, pages 655–665, Baltimore, Maryland, USA.

Yoon Kim. 2014. Convolutional Neural Networks for Sentence Classification. In *Proceedings of EMNLP-2014*, pages 1746–1751, Doha, Quatar.

Klaus Krippendorff. 2007. Computing Krippendorff's alpha reliability. *Departmental papers (ASC)*, page 43.

Marco Lui and Timothy Baldwin. 2012. langid. py: An off-the-shelf language identification tool. In *Proceedings of the ACL 2012 system demonstrations*, pages 25–30, Jeju Island, Korea.

Eugenio Martinez-Camara, M. Teresa Martin-Valdivia, L. Alfonso Urena-Lopez, and Ruslan Mitkov. 2015. Polarity classification for Spanish tweets using the COST corpus. *Journal of Information Science*, 41(3):263–272.

Eugenio Martinez-Camara, Miguel A. Garcia-Cumbreras, Julio Villena-Roman, and Janine Garcia-Morera. 2016. TASS 2015 - The Evolution of the Spanish Opinion Mining Systems. *Procesamiento del Lenguaje Natural*, 56:33–40.

Igor Mozetič, Miha Grčar, and Jasmina Smailović. 2016. Multilingual Twitter Sentiment Classification: The Role of Human Annotators. *PloS one*, 11(5):e0155036.

Preslav Nakov, Alan Ritter, Sara Rosenthal, Fabrizio Sebastiani, and Veselin Stoyanov. 2016. SemEval-2016 task 4: Sentiment analysis in Twitter. In *Proceedings of SemEval-2016*, pages 1–18, San Diego, USA.

Sascha Narr, Michael Hulfenhaus, and Sahin Albayrak. 2012. Language-independent twitter sentiment analysis. *Knowledge Discovery and Machine Learning (KDML), LWA*, pages 12–14.

Iadh Ounis, Craig Macdonald, and Ian Soboroff. 2008. Overview of the TREC-2008 Blog Track. In *Proceedings of TREC-2008*.

Jonathon Read. 2005. Using emoticons to reduce dependency in machine learning techniques for sentiment classification. In *Proceedings of the ACL student research workshop*, pages 43–48, Ann Arbor, Michigan.

Sara Rosenthal, Alan Ritter, Preslav Nakov, and Veselin Stoyanov. 2014. SemEval-2014 task 9: Sentiment analysis in Twitter. In *Proceedings of SemEval-2014*, pages 73 – 80, Dublin, Ireland.

Sara Rosenthal, Preslav Nakov, Svetlana Kiritchenko, Saif M Mohammad, Alan Ritter, and Veselin Stoyanov. 2015. Semeval-2015 task 10: Sentiment analysis in twitter. *Proceedings of SemEval-2015*, pages 451–463.

Sascha Rothe, Sebastian Ebert, and Hinrich Schutze. 2016. Ultradense Word Embeddings by Orthogonal Transformation. *arXiv*.

Josef Ruppenhofer, Roman Klinger, Julia Maria Struß, Jonathan Sonntag, and Michael Wiegand. 2014. IGGSA Shared Tasks on German Sentiment Analysis (GESTALT). In *Workshop Proceedings of the 12th*

Edition of the KONVENS Conference, pages 164 – 173, Hildesheim, Germany.

Aliaksei Severyn and Alessandro Moschitti. 2015. UNITN: Training Deep Convolutional Neural Network for Twitter Sentiment Classification. In *Proceedings of SemEval-2015*, pages 464–469, Denver, Colorado.

Yelong Shen, Xiaodong He, Jianfeng Gao, Li Deng, and Grégoire Mesnil. 2014. A latent semantic model with convolutional-pooling structure for information retrieval. In *Proceedings of the 23rd ACM International Conference on Conference on Information and Knowledge Management*, pages 101–110, Shanghai, China.

Uladzimir Sidarenka. 2016. PotTS: The Potsdam Twitter Sentiment Corpus. In *Proceedings of LREC-2016*, pages 1133 – 1141, Portoroz, Slovenia.

Richard Socher, Alex Perelygin, Jean Y Wu, Jason Chuang, Christopher D Manning, Andrew Y Ng, and Christopher Potts. 2013. Recursive deep models for semantic compositionality over a sentiment treebank. In *Proceedings of EMNLP-2013*, volume 1631, page 1642, Seattle, Washington, USA.

Marco Straniscim, Christina Bosco, Delia Irazu Hernnandez Farias, and Viviana Patti. 2016. Annotating Sentiment and Irony in the Online Italian Political Debate on labuonascuola. In *Proceedings of LREC-2016*, pages 2892–2899, Portoroz, Slovenia.

Fatih Uzdilli, Martin Jaggi, Dominic Egger, Pascal Julmy, Leon Derczynski, and Mark Cieliebak. 2015. Swiss-Chocolate: Combining Flipout Regularization and Random Forests with Artificially Built Subsystems to Boost Text-Classification for Sentiment. In *Proceedings of SemEval-2015*, pages 608–612, Denver, Colorado.

Ben Verhoeven and Walter Daelemans. 2014. CLiPS Stylometry Investigation (CSI) corpus: A Dutch corpus for the detection of age, gender, personality, sentiment and deception in text. In *Proceedings of LREC-2014*, pages 3081–3085, Reykjavik, Iceland.

Ulli Waltinger. 2010. GermanPolarityClues: A Lexical Resource for German Sentiment Analysis. In *Proceedings of LREC-2010*, pages 1638–1642, Valletta, Malta.

Janyce Wiebe, Theresa Wilson, and Claire Cardie. 2005. Annotating expressions of opinions and emotions in language. *Language resources and evaluation*, 39(2-3):165–210.

Jun Zhao, Kang Liu, and Liheng Xu. 2016. *Sentiment Analysis: Mining Opinions, Sentiments, and Emotions*. MIT Press, Cambridge, MA, USA.

Author Index

Association for Computational Linguistics
209 N. Eighth Street
Stroudsburg, Pennsylvania 18360

ISBN 978-1-5108-3871-0

9 781510 838710

CURRAN ASSOCIATES INC.
proceedings.com